THE
BELIEVER'S
WALK WITH
CHRIST

THE BELIEVER'S WALK WITH CHRIST

THE JOHN MACARTHUR STUDY SERIES

JOHN MACARTHUR

MOODY PUBLISHERS

CHICAGO

THE MASTER'S SEMINARY PRESS

LOS ANGELES

Unless otherwise indicated, Scripture quotations are from the New American Standard Bible®, Copyright © 1960, 1962, 1963, 1968, 1971, 1972, 1973, 1975, 1977, 1995 by The Lockman Foundation. Used by permission. (www.Lockman.org)

Scripture quotations marked NIV are taken from the Holy Bible, New International Version®, NIV®. Copyright © 1973, 1978, 1984, 2011 by Biblica, Inc.™ *Used by permission of Zondervan. All rights reserved worldwide.* www.zondervan.com. The "NIV" and "New International Version" are trademarks registered in the United States Patent and Trademark Office by Biblica, Inc.™

Scripture quotations marked KJV are taken from the King James Version.

Scripture quotations marked NKJV are taken from the New King James Version. Copyright © 1982 by Thomas Nelson. Used by permission. All rights reserved.

All websites listed herein are accurate at the time of publication but may change in the future or cease to exist. The listing of website references and resources does not imply publisher endorsement of the site's entire contents.

Edited by: Jim Vincent
Interior design: Ragont Design
Cover design: Erik M. Peterson
Cover image of men walking copyright © 2016 by Pearl /Lightstock (79930)

Library of Congress Cataloging-in-Publication Data

Names: MacArthur, John, 1939- author.
Title: The believer's walk with Christ / John MacArthur.
Description: Chicago : Moody Publishers, 2017. | Series: The John MacArthur study series
Identifiers: LCCN 2016045847 (print) | LCCN 2016047252 (ebook) | ISBN 9780802415196 | ISBN 9780802495280 ()
Subjects: LCSH: Christian life--Biblical teaching.
Classification: LCC BS2545.C48 M33 2017 (print) | LCC BS2545.C48 (ebook) | DDC 248.4--dc23
LC record available at https://lccn.loc.gov/2016045847

We hope you enjoy this book from Moody Publishers. Our goal is to provide high-quality, thought-provoking books and products that connect truth to your real needs and challenges. For more information on other books and products written and produced from a biblical perspective, go to www.moodypublishers.com or write to:

Moody Publishers
820 N. LaSalle Boulevard
Chicago, IL 60610

1a 3 5 7 9 10 8 6 4 2

Printed in the United States of America

About This Series

This volume is part of *The John MacArthur Study Series*. It is comprised of chapters adapted from *The MacArthur New Testament Commentary*, which have been arranged thematically for the purpose of topical study. Accordingly, each chapter is designed to take the reader down deep into the text of Scripture; while the volume as a whole addresses a specific biblical theme.

This approach is ideal for anyone wanting to engage in an in-depth study of what the Bible says about a given subject. It also serves as a valuable tool for pastors or Bible study leaders looking to teach a series on this important topic.

CONTENTS

PREFACE

W alking" is a rich biblical metaphor, used in Scripture to describe a person's pursuits and patterns of behavior. In the Old Testament, those who walked with God—like Enoch (Gen. 5:22–24), Noah (Gen. 6:9), Abraham (Gen. 17:1), David (1 Kings 3:14), Hezekiah (2 Kings 20:3), and Josiah (2 Kings 22:2)—were characterized by both earnest love for Him and joyful obedience to His Word. Out of their passion to pursue God, they sought to live in a way that pleased Him (cf. Deut. 8:6; 10:12). Their lives were characterized by patterns of integrity (Ps. 15:2), uprightness (Prov. 14:2), wisdom (Prov. 28:26), and conformity to His Word (Ps. 119:1, 35), while they avoided the treacherous ways of the wicked (Ps. 1:1; Prov. 4:14).

The theme of walking also appears in the New Testament, as the apostle Paul commands believers to no longer walk according to the flesh (Rom. 8:4) or their old manner of behavior (Eph. 4:17). Instead, Christians are to walk in newness of life (Rom. 6:4), by the power of the Holy Spirit (Gal. 5:16, 25). Because they are new creatures in Christ (2 Cor. 5:17), their walk (or way of life) is to be characterized by faith (2 Cor. 5:7), good works (Eph. 2:10), humility (Eph. 4:1–3), love (Eph. 5:2), holiness (Eph. 5:8), wisdom (Eph. 5:15), truth (2 John 4), and obedience (2 John 6). Consequently, believers are instructed to "walk in a manner worthy of the God who calls you into His own kingdom and glory" (1 Thess. 2:12); to "walk in a manner worthy of the calling with which you have been called" (Eph. 4:1); and to "conduct yourselves in a manner worthy of the gospel of Christ" (Phil. 1:27).

But what does it mean, as a Christian, to walk in a manner

worthy of our calling? In order to answer that question, we are going to examine nine New Testament passages that delineate different aspects of the believer's walk with Christ (i.e., the Christian life). My prayer for you, as you work your way through the subsequent pages, is reflected in Paul's words to the Colossians:

> We have not ceased to pray for you and to ask that you may be filled with the knowledge of His will in all spiritual wisdom and understanding, so that you will walk in a manner worthy of the Lord, to please Him in all respects, bearing fruit in every good work and increasing in the knowledge of God. (Col. 1:9–10)

Chapter 1

WALKING WORTHY OF THE GOSPEL

EPHESIANS 4:1–6

Therefore I, the prisoner of the Lord, implore you to walk in a manner worthy of the calling with which you have been called, with all humility and gentleness, with patience, showing tolerance for one another in love, being diligent to preserve the unity of the Spirit in the bond of peace. There is one body and one Spirit, just as also you were called in one hope of your calling; one Lord, one faith, one baptism, one God and Father of all who is over all and through all and in all. (4:1–6)

When a person joins an organization, he obligates himself to live and act in accordance with the standards of the group. He accepts its aims, objectives, and standards as his own. A citizen is obligated to abide by the laws of his country. An employee is obligated to work according to the rules, standards, and purposes of his company. When someone joins an athletic team he is obligated to play as the coach orders and according to the rules of the sport. Human society could not operate without such obligations.

We have a natural desire to be accepted and to belong, and many people will go to almost any lengths to qualify for acceptance in a fraternal order, social club, athletic team, or other group. Many people will also go to great lengths to keep from being rejected by a group. The parents of the man born blind were afraid to tell the Jewish leaders that Jesus had healed their son, because they were afraid of being thrown out of the synagogue (John 9:22). Although they had seen the result of a miracle that had healed their own son of his lifelong blindness, they would not credit Jesus with the miracle for fear of being socially ostracized. For the same reason, "many even of the rulers believed in Him, but . . . were not confessing Him, lest they should be put out of the synagogue; for they loved the approval of men rather than the approval of God" (12:42–43).

Sometimes in the church such loyalties to standards and fear of ostracism do not operate with the same force. Too many Christians are glad to have the spiritual security, blessings, and promises of the gospel but have too little sense of responsibility in conforming to its standards and obeying its commands.

In the first three chapters of Ephesians Paul has set forth the believer's position with all the blessings, honors, and privileges of being a child of God. In the next three chapters he gives the consequent obligations and requirements of being His child, in order to live out salvation in accordance with the Father's will and to His glory. The first three chapters set forth truth about the believer's identity in Christ, and the last three call for the practical response.

When we received Christ as Savior we became citizens of His kingdom and members of His family. Along with those blessings and privileges we also received obligations. The Lord expects us to act like the new persons we have become in Jesus Christ. He expects His standards to become our standards, His purposes our purposes, His desires our desires, His nature our nature. The Christian life is simply the process of becoming what you are.

God expects conformity within the church, the body of Christ. It is not a forced legalistic conformity to external rules and regulations, but a willing inner conformity to the holiness, love, and will of our heavenly Father, who wants His children to honor Him as their Father. "Conduct yourselves in a manner worthy of the gospel of Christ," Paul admonished the Philippians, "so that whether I come and see you or remain absent, I will hear of you that you are standing firm in one spirit, with one mind striving together for the faith of the gospel" (Phil. 1:27).

The "therefore" of Ephesians 4:1 marks the transition from positional to practical truth, from doctrine to duty, from principle to practice. Paul makes a similar transition in the book of Romans. After laying down eleven chapters of doctrine, he devotes the remainder of the book to urging Christians to live in accordance with that doctrine—to present their bodies as "a living and holy sacrifice, acceptable to God, which is your spiritual service of worship" (12:1). In Galatians Paul devotes the first four chapters to explaining Christian liberty and the last two chapters to exhorting Christians to live by that liberty. That sort of division is found in many of Paul's epistles (see also Phil. 2:1–2; Col. 3:5; 1 Thess. 4:1). Right practice must always be based on right principle. It is impossible to have a Christian lifestyle without knowing the realities of the life that Christ has provided.

Right doctrine is essential to right living. It is impossible to live a faithful Christian life without knowing biblical doctrine. Doctrine simply means teaching, and there is no way that even the most sincere believer can live a life pleasing to God without knowing what God Himself is like and knowing the sort of life God wants him to live. Those who set biblical theology aside also set aside sound Christian living.

Church renewal does not come with new programs, buildings, organization, educational methods, or anything else external. Church renewal comes first of all through the renewal of the mind. Later in this letter Paul prays that the Ephesians would "be renewed in the spirit of your mind, and put on the new self, which in the likeness of God has been created in righteousness and holiness of the truth" (4:23–24). It is only when in the spirit of their minds they grasp the righteousness and holiness of God's truth that God's people are renewed. At the beginning of this letter Paul prayed "that the God of our Lord Jesus Christ, the Father of glory, may give to you a spirit of wisdom and of revelation in the knowledge of Him" (1:17). Growing in grace, Peter tells us, is linked with growing in the "knowledge of our Lord and Savior Jesus Christ" (2 Pet. 3:18). Along with his ministry of proclaiming Christ, Paul also was "admonishing every man and teaching every man with all wisdom, so that we may present every man complete in Christ" (Col. 1:28). It is impossible to do good works without knowledge of the Word of God (2 Tim. 3:16–17).

THE CALL TO THE WORTHY WALK

Therefore I, the prisoner of the Lord, implore you to walk in a manner worthy of the calling with which you have been called, (4:1)

Before giving his appeal, Paul once again refers to himself as "the prisoner of the Lord" (see 3:1). By mentioning his imprisonment he gently reminds his readers that he knows the worthy Christian walk can be costly and that he has paid considerable cost himself because of his obedience to the Lord. He would not ask them to walk in a way in which he had not himself walked or pay a price that he himself was not willing to pay. His present physical circumstance seemed extremely negative from a human perspective, but Paul wanted his readers to know that this did not change his commitment to, nor his confidence in, the Lord.

The apostle was not seeking sympathy or using his Roman confinement as a means for shaming the Ephesians into compliance with his request. He was reminding them again of his own complete subservience to Christ, his being the prisoner of the Lord whether he was in jail or not. He became the Lord's prisoner on the road to Damascus and never sought to be free of that divine imprisonment.

Paul had the ability to see everything in the light of how it affected Christ. He saw everything vertically before he saw it horizontally. His motives were Christ's, his standards were Christ's, his objectives were Christ's, his vision was Christ's—his entire orientation was Christ's. Everything he thought, planned, said, and did was in relation to his Lord. He was in the fullest sense a captive of the Lord Jesus Christ.

Most of us will admit that we tend to be so self-oriented that we see many things first of all—and sometimes only—in relation to ourselves. But the person who has the Word of Christ abiding in him richly, the one who saturates his or her mind with divine wisdom and truth will ask, "How does this affect God? How will it reflect on Him? What does He want me to do with this problem or this blessing? How can I most please and honor Him in this?" That person tries to see everything through God's divine grid. Such an attitude is the basis and the mark of spiritual maturity. With David, the mature Christian can say, "I have set the Lord continually before me; because He is at my right hand" (Ps. 16:8).

Paul made no apology for pleading with people to do what

he knew was right. "I . . . implore you," he says. The Greek word *parakaleō* (translated "implore") means to call to one's side, with the idea of wanting to help or be helped. It connotes intense feeling, strong desire. In this context it is not simply a request but a plea, almost a begging. Paul was not giving suggestions to the Ephesians but divine standards, standards apart from which they could not live in a way that fittingly corresponded to their being children of God. Paul never exhorted on a take-it-or-leave-it basis. He could not rest until all those given into his spiritual care walked "in a manner worthy of the calling" with which they had been called.

Paul pleaded with King Agrippa to listen to his testimony (Acts 26:3), he strongly urged the Corinthians to reaffirm their love for a repentant brother (2 Cor. 2:8), and pleaded with the Galatians to stand in the liberty of the gospel as he did (Gal. 4:12). He pleaded out of an intense love for others, saved and unsaved. Of unsaved fellow Jews, he wrote, "I am telling the truth in Christ, I am not lying, my conscience testifies with me in the Holy Spirit, that I have great sorrow and unceasing grief in my heart. For I could wish that I myself were accursed, separated from Christ for the sake of my brethren, my kinsmen according to the flesh" (Rom. 9:1–3).

Christians should not resent a pastor's entreating them in the faith as Paul did those to whom he ministered. A pastor who approaches his ministry with detachment or indifference is not worthy of his office. Loving concern for the spiritual welfare of others is costly, and apart from God's strength it is frustrating and demoralizing.

Not only pastors but all believers should have a loving concern to implore, entreat, beg, and plead with others to respond in obedience to the gospel. Like Paul, they should have a passion to implore their fellow believers to walk in a manner worthy of their calling—to be everything the Lord desires of them.

"Walk" is frequently used in the New Testament to refer to daily conduct, day-by-day living, and it is the theme of the last three chapters of Ephesians. In the first sixteen verses of chapter 4, Paul emphasizes the unity and in the rest of the chapter the uniqueness of the Christian walk. In chapters 5 and 6 he stresses the moral purity, the wisdom, the Spirit control, the family manifestations, and the warfare of the Christian walk.

The Greek word for "worthy," *axios*, has the root meaning of balancing the scales—what is on one side of the scale should be equal in weight to what is on the other side. By extension, the word came to be applied to anything that was expected to correspond to something else. A person worthy of his pay was one whose day's work corresponded to his day's wages. The believer who walks "in a manner worthy of the calling" with which he has been called is one whose daily living corresponds to his high position as a child of God and fellow heir with Jesus Christ. His practical living matches his spiritual position.

This calling is the sovereign, saving calling of God (cf. 1 Thess. 2:12). Paul tells us that those whom God "predestined, He also called; and these whom He called, He also justified; and . . . whom He justified, He also glorified" (Rom. 8:30). As the apostle mentioned in the opening of this letter, "He chose us in Him before the foundation of the world, that we would be holy and blameless before Him" (Eph. 1:4). No person can be saved apart from receiving Jesus Christ as his Savior. But no person can choose Christ who has not already been chosen by the Father and the Son. "You did not choose Me," Jesus explained to the disciples, "but I chose you, and appointed you that you would go and bear fruit, and that your fruit would remain" (John 15:16).

Paul makes many references to the believer's calling (*klēsis*), which, as in this case, refers to the Lord's sovereign, effectual call to salvation (Rom. 11:29; 1 Cor. 1:26; Eph. 1:18; 4:1, 4; Phil. 3:14; 2 Thess. 1:11; 2 Tim. 1:9; cf. Heb. 3:1; 2 Pet. 1:10).

Without God's calling, without His choosing us, our choosing Him would be futile. In fact, if God did not call men to Himself no man would *want* to come to Him, because the natural man—every natural man—is at enmity with God (Rom. 8:7). The marvelous truth of the gospel is that God not only sent His Son to *provide* the way of salvation (Rom. 5:8) but that He sent Him to *seek* the lost in order to save them (Luke 19:10). God was not content simply to make salvation available. He has called the redeemed elect to Himself.

That is why our **calling** is a high calling, a "heavenly calling" (Heb. 3:1), and "a holy calling" (2 Tim. 1:9). And that is why the faithful, responsive Christian is determined to "press on toward the goal for the prize of the upward call of God in Christ Jesus" (Phil. 3:14).

THE CHARACTERISTICS
OF THE WORTHY WALK

with all humility and gentleness, with patience, showing tolerance for one another in love, being diligent to preserve the unity of the Spirit in the bond of peace. (4:2–3)

Here Paul gives five essentials for faithful Christian living, five attitudes on which walking worthily in the Lord's call are predicated.

1. Humility

These characteristics, of which humility is the foundation, form a progression, the genuine exercise of one leading to the exercise of those that follow.

Tapeinophrosunē ("humility") is a compound word that literally means to think or judge with lowliness, and hence to have lowliness of mind. John Wesley observed that "neither the Romans nor the Greeks had a word for humility." The very concept was so foreign and abhorrent to their way of thinking that they had no term to describe it. Apparently this Greek term was coined by Christians, probably by Paul himself, to describe a quality for which no other word was available. To the proud Greeks and Romans, their terms for ignoble, cowardly, and other such characteristics were sufficient to describe the "unnatural" person who did not think of himself with pride and self-satisfaction. When, during the first several centuries of Christianity, pagan writers borrowed the term *tapeinophrosunē*, they always used it derogatorily—frequently of Christians—because to them humility was a pitiable weakness.

But humility is the most foundational Christian virtue. We cannot even begin to please God without humility, just as our Lord Himself could not have pleased His Father had He not willingly "emptied Himself, taking the form of a bond-servant, and . . . humbled Himself by becoming obedient to the point of death, even death on a cross" (Phil. 2:7–8).

Yet humility is terribly elusive, because if focused on too much it will turn into pride, its very opposite. Humility is a virtue to be highly sought but never claimed, because once claimed it is forfeited. Only Jesus Christ, as the perfectly obedient Son, could justifiably claim humility for Himself. "Take My yoke upon you," He said, "for I am gentle and humble in heart" (Matt. 11:29). He came to earth as God's Son, yet was born in a stable, raised in a peasant family, never owned property except the garments on His back, and was buried in a borrowed tomb. At any time He could have exercised His divine rights, prerogatives, and glory, but in obedience and humility He refused to do so because it would have been to go outside His Father's will. If the Lord of glory walked in humility while He was on earth, how much more are His imperfect followers to do so? "The one who says he abides in Him ought himself to walk in the same manner as He walked" (1 John 2:6).

Although humility is at the heart of Christian character, no virtue is more foreign to the world's ways. The world exalts pride, not humility. Throughout history, fallen human nature, ruled by Satan, the prince of this world, has shunned humility and advocated pride. For the most part humility has been looked on as weakness and impotence, something ignoble to be despised. People unashamedly claim to be proud of their jobs, their children, their accomplishments, and on and on. Society loves to recognize and praise those who have accomplished something outstanding. Ostentation, boasting, parading, and exalting are the world's stock in trade.

Unfortunately the church often reflects that worldly perspective and pattern, building many programs and organizations around the superficial enticements of awards, trophies, and public recognition. We seem to have found a way to encourage boasting that is "acceptable," because such boasting is done in the name of the gospel. But in doing so we contradict the very gospel we claim to promote, because the hallmark of the gospel is humility, not pride and self-exaltation. God's work cannot be served by the world's ways. God's call is to humility and His work is only accomplished *through* humility.

HUMILITY VERSUS PRIDE (THE FIRST SIN)

The first sin was pride, and every sin after that has been in some way an extension of pride. Pride led the angel Lucifer to exalt himself above his Creator and Lord. Because the bright "star of the morning" continually said, "I will, I will, I will" in opposition to God's will, he was cast out of heaven (Isa. 14:12–23). Because he said, "I am a god," the Lord cast him "from the mountain of God" (Ezek. 28:11–19). The original sin of Adam and Eve was pride, trusting in their own understanding above God's (Gen. 3:6–7). The writer of Proverbs warns, "When pride comes, then comes dishonor" (Prov. 11:2), "Pride goes before destruction, and a haughty spirit before stumbling" (16:18), and again "Haughty eyes and a proud heart, the lamp of the wicked, is sin" (21:4).

As believers, our only protection against pride, and our only source of humility, is a proper view of God. Pride is the sin of competing with God, and humility is the virtue of submitting to His supreme glory. Thus James warns us, "God is opposed to the proud, but gives grace to the humble" (James 4:6; cf. Ps. 138:6).

Pride comes in many forms. We may be tempted to be proud of our abilities, our possessions, our education, our social status, our appearance, our power, and even our biblical knowledge or religious accomplishments. But throughout Scripture the Lord calls His people to humility. "Before honor comes humility" (Prov. 15:33); "The reward of humility and the fear of the Lord are riches, honor and life" (22:4); "Let another praise you, and not your own mouth; a stranger, and not your own lips" (27:2).

HUMILITY: A PART OF SPIRITUAL BLESSINGS

Humility is an ingredient of all spiritual blessings. Just as every sin has its roots in pride, every virtue has its roots in humility. Humility allows us to see ourselves as we are, because it shows us before God as He is. Just as pride is behind every conflict we have with other people and every problem of fellowship we have with the Lord, so humility is behind every harmonious human relationship, every spiritual success, and every moment of joyous fellowship with the Lord.

During the days of slavery in the West Indies, a group of Moravian settlers found it difficult to reach out to the slaves, who were almost totally separated from the ruling class. Many of the Moravians proudly felt it beneath them even to speak to a slave. Two young missionaries, however, were determined to reach those oppressed peoples at any cost. In order to fulfill God's calling they joined the slaves. They worked and lived beside the slaves, becoming totally identified with them—sharing their overwork, their beatings, and their abuse. It is not strange that the two missionaries soon won the hearts of those slaves, many of whom accepted for themselves the God who could move men to such loving selflessness.

A person cannot even become a Christian without humility, without recognizing himself as a sinner and worthy only of God's just condemnation. "Truly I say to you," Jesus said, "unless you are converted and become like children, you will not enter the kingdom of heaven. Whoever then humbles himself . . ." (Matt. 18:3–4). At the height of his own fame and recognition as a prophet, John the Baptist said of Jesus, "I am not fit to remove His sandals" (Matt. 3:11) and "He must increase, but I must decrease" (John 3:30). Martha was busy doing many things supposedly for Jesus' sake, but on three different occasions we see Mary simply sitting humbly at Jesus' feet.

In all four Gospels the writers hide themselves and focus attention on Jesus. How easy it would have been for them to subtly include accounts favorable to themselves. Matthew identifies himself as a despised tax collector, which none of the other gospel writers does. On the other hand, he does not mention the feast that he gave for his fellow tax collectors to meet Jesus. Because of Matthew's humility, it was left to Luke to write about that. Mark probably wrote under the tutelage of Peter, and possibly because of that apostle's influence he does not report two of the most amazing things that happened to Peter during Jesus' ministry—his walking on water and his confession of Jesus as the Christ, the Son of the living God. John never mentions his own name, referring to himself simply as "the disciple whom Jesus loved." In a compilation of old quotes is an excellent paragraph written by Thomas Guthrie:

> The grandest edifices, the tallest towers, the loftiest spires rest on deep foundations. The very safety of eminent gifts and preeminent graces lies in their association with deep humility. They are dangerous without it. Great men do need to be good men. Look at the mighty ship. A leviathan into the sea, with her towering masts and carrying a cloud of canvas. How she steadies herself on the waves and walks erect on the rolling waters like a thing with inherent, self-regulating life. . . . Why is she not flung on her beam's end, sent down floundering into the deep? Because unseen beneath the surface a vast well-ballasted hull gives her balance and takes hold of the water, keeps her steady under a pressive sail and on the bosom of a swelling sea. Even though to preserve the saint upright, to preserve the saint erect and safe from falling, God gives him balance and ballast bestowing on the man to whom He has given lofty endowments, the [attending] grace of a proportionate humility.

Humility begins with proper self-awareness, "the virtue," said Bernard of Clairvaux, "by which a man becomes conscious of his own unworthiness." It begins with an honest, unadorned, unretouched view of oneself. The first thing the honest person sees in himself is sin, and therefore one of the surest marks of true humility is daily confession of sin. "If we say that we have no sin, we are deceiving ourselves and the truth is not in us. If we confess our sins, He is faithful and righteous to forgive us our sins and to cleanse us from all unrighteousness" (1 John 1:8–9). "We are not bold to class or compare ourselves with some of those who commend themselves," Paul says; "but when they measure themselves by themselves and compare themselves with themselves, they are without understanding" (2 Cor. 10:12). It is not only unspiritual but unintelligent to judge ourselves by comparison with others. We all tend to exaggerate our own good qualities and minimize the good qualities of others. Humility takes off our rose-colored glasses and allows us to see ourselves as we really are. We are not "adequate in ourselves to consider anything as coming from ourselves," says Paul, "but our adequacy is from God" (2 Cor. 3:5).

Second, humility involves Christ-awareness. He is the only standard by which righteousness can be judged and by which pleasing God can be judged. Our goal should be no less than "to walk in the same manner as He walked" (1 John 2:6), and Jesus Christ walked in perfection. Only of Jesus has God ever said, "This is My beloved Son, in whom I am well-pleased" (Matt. 3:17).

Third, humility involves God-awareness. As we study His life in the Gospels we come to see Jesus more and more in His human perfection—His perfect humility, His perfect submission to the Father, His perfect love, compassion, and wisdom. But beyond His human perfection we also come to see His divine perfection—His limitless power; His knowing the thoughts and heart of every person; and His authority to heal diseases, cast out demons, and even forgive sins. We come to see Jesus Christ as Isaiah saw the Lord, "sitting on a throne, lofty and exalted" and we want to cry out with the seraphim, "Holy, Holy, Holy, is the Lord of hosts, the whole earth is full of His glory," and with the prophet himself, "Woe is me, for I am ruined! Because I am a man of unclean lips, and I live among a people of unclean lips; for my eyes have seen the King, the Lord of hosts" (Isa. 6:1, 3, 5).

When Paul looked at himself in self-awareness, he saw the foremost of sinners (1 Tim. 1:15). When Peter looked at himself in Christ awareness, he said, "Go away from me Lord, for I am a sinful man!" (Luke 5:8). When Job looked at himself in God awareness, he said, "Therefore I retract, and I repent in dust and ashes" (Job 42:6).

Our business success, fame, education, wealth, personality, good works, or anything else we are or have in ourselves counts for nothing before God. The more we rely on and glory in such things, the greater barrier they become to our communion with God. Every person comes before the Lord with nothing to commend him and everything to condemn him. But when he comes with the spirit of the penitent tax collector, saying, "God, be merciful to me, the sinner," God will willingly and lovingly accept him. "For everyone who exalts himself will be humbled, but he who humbles himself will be exalted" (Luke 18:13–14).

2. *Gentleness*

Humility always produces gentleness, or meekness. Meekness is one of the surest signs of true humility. You cannot possess meekness *without* humility, and you cannot possess meekness *with* pride.

25

Because pride and humility are mutually exclusive, so are pride and meekness, or gentleness.

THE NATURE OF GENTLENESS

Many dictionaries define meekness in terms such as "timid," or "a deficiency in courage or spirit"; but that is far from the biblical meaning. *Praotēs* (here translated "gentleness") refers to that which is mild-spirited and self-controlled, the opposite of vindictiveness and vengeance. Jesus used the adjective form in giving the third beatitude ("Blessed are the gentle," Matt. 5:5) and to describe His own character ("For I am gentle," Matt. 11:29). Gentleness is one of the fruits of the Spirit (Gal. 5:23) and should characterize every child of God (Col. 3:12; cf. Phil. 4:5).

The meaning of *praotēs* has nothing to do with weakness, timidity, indifference, or cowardice. It was used of wild animals that were tamed, especially of horses that were broken and trained. Such an animal still has his strength and spirit, but his will is under the control of his master. The tamed lion is still powerful, but his power is under the control of his trainer. The horse can run just as fast, but he runs only when and where his master tells him to run.

EXAMPLES OF BIBLICAL MEEKNESS

Meekness is power under control. Biblical meekness, or "gentleness," is power under the control of God. A meek person is normally quiet, soothing, and mild mannered, and he is never avenging, self-assertive, vindictive, or self-defensive. When the soldiers came to arrest Him in the garden of Gethsemane and Peter drew his sword to defend His Lord, Jesus said, "Do you think that I cannot appeal to My Father, and He will at once put at My disposal more than twelve legions of angels?" (Matt. 26:53). Even in His humanity Jesus had access to infinite divine power, which He could at any time have used in His own defense. Yet not once did He choose to do so. His refusal to enlist divine resources for anything but obeying His Father's will is the supreme picture of meekness—power under control.

David displayed such meekness when he refused to kill King Saul in the cave near Engedi, although he had easy opportunity and considerable justification from the human point of view (1 Sam. 24:1–7). After David himself became king, he again showed the restraint of meekness when he refused to retaliate against the malicious taunts, curses, and stone throwing of Shimei (2 Sam. 16:5–14).

Moses is described as "very humble, more than any man who was on the face of the earth" (Num. 12:3). Yet he fearlessly confronted Pharaoh in the Lord's name (see Ex. 5–12), angrily confronted Israel with her rebelliousness and idolatry (32:19–29), and even boldly confronted the Lord to forgive the people's sin (32:11–13, 30–32). Yet Moses's confidence was not in himself but in the Lord's character and promises. When God first called him, Moses replied, "Please, Lord, I have never been eloquent, neither recently nor in time past, nor since You have spoken to Your servant; for I am slow of speech and slow of tongue" (4:10). As he served the Lord throughout his life, Moses had God's rod to remind him that the great work to which the Lord had called him could be accomplished only in the Lord's own power. That he himself was nothing and God was everything were the marks of Moses's meekness. As Martyn Lloyd-Jones has observed, "To be meek means you have finished with yourself altogether."

Yet the meek person is also capable of righteous anger and action when God's Word or name is maligned, as Jesus was when His Father's house was made into a robber's den and He forcibly drove out the offenders (Matt. 21:13). As Paul affirms later in this letter, it is possible to be angry and not sin (Eph. 4:26). Like the Lord Himself, the meek person does not revile in return when he is reviled (1 Peter 2:23). When the meek person becomes angry, he is aroused by that which maligns God or is harmful to others, not by what is done against himself. And his anger is controlled and carefully directed, not a careless and wild venting of emotion that spatters everyone who is near.

THE CHARACTER OF THE MEEK AND GENTLE

One of the marks of true meekness is self-control. People who are angered at every nuisance or inconvenience to themselves know nothing of meekness or gentleness. "He who is slow to anger is better than the mighty, and he who rules his spirit, than he who captures a city" (Prov. 16:32). Two other marks of meekness, already mentioned, are anger at God's name or work being maligned and *lack* of anger when we ourselves are harmed or criticized.

The meek person responds willingly to the Word of God, no matter what the requirements or consequences, humbly receiving "the word implanted" (James 1:21). He is also a peacemaker, who readily forgives and helps to restore a sinning brother (Gal. 6:1). Finally, the person who is truly meek and gentle according to God's standards has the right attitude toward the unsaved. He does not look down on them with a feeling of superiority but longs for their salvation, knowing that he himself was once lost—and would still be lost but for God's grace. We are to be "ready to make a defense to everyone who asks [us] to give an account for the hope that is in [us], yet with gentleness [*praotēs*] and reverence" (1 Pet. 3:15). Not only Christian women but all believers should be adorned "with the imperishable quality of a gentle and quiet spirit" (1 Peter 3:4).

3. Patience

A third attitude that characterizes the Christian's worthy walk is patience, which is an outgrowth of humility and gentleness. *Makrothurmia* ("patience") literally means long-tempered, and is sometimes translated "longsuffering." The patient person endures negative circumstances and never gives in to them.

BIBLICAL EXAMPLES OF PATIENCE

Abraham received the promise of God but had to wait many years to see its fulfillment. "Thus," the writer of Hebrews tells us, "having patiently waited, he obtained the promise" (Heb. 6:15). God had promised that Abraham's descendants would be a great nation (Gen. 12:2) and yet he was not given Isaac, the child of promise, until after Abraham was nearly a hundred years old. "Yet, with respect to the promise of God, he did not waver in unbelief but grew strong in faith, giving glory to God" (Rom. 4:20).

God told Noah to build a ship in the wilderness, far from any body of water and before there had ever been rain on earth. For 120 years Noah worked at that task, while preaching to his neighbors of God's coming judgment.

In the chronicle of faithful Old Testament saints in the book of Hebrews, Moses's patient endurance is mentioned twice. He chose rather "to endure ill-treatment with the people of God than to enjoy the passing pleasures of sin, considering the reproach of Christ greater riches than the treasures of Egypt; for he was looking to the reward. By faith he left Egypt, not fearing the wrath of the king; for he endured, as seeing Him who is unseen" (Heb. 11:25–27).

James said, "As an example, brethren, of suffering and patience, take the prophets who spoke in the name of the Lord" (James

5:10). When God called Jeremiah, He told the prophet that no one would believe his message and that he would be hated, maligned, and persecuted (Jer. 1:5–19). Yet Jeremiah served the Lord faithfully and patiently until the end of his life. Similarly, when the Lord called Isaiah he was told that the nation would not listen to him nor turn from their sin (Isa. 6:9–12). Like Jeremiah, however, he preached and ministered with patient faithfulness.

Paul was willing to endure any hardship, affliction, ridicule, or persecution in order to patiently serve his Master. "What are you doing, weeping and breaking my heart?" he asked the Christians at Caesarea after the prophet Agabus predicted the apostle's arrest and imprisonment. "For I am ready not only to be bound, but even to die at Jerusalem for the name of the Lord Jesus" (Acts 21:13).

THE IMPACT OF PATIENCE: DR. LIVINGSTONE

When H. M. Stanley went to Africa in 1871 to find and report on David Livingstone, he spent several months in the missionary's company, carefully observing the man and his work. Livingstone never spoke to Stanley about spiritual matters, but Livingstone's loving and patient compassion for the African people was beyond Stanley's comprehension. He could not understand how the missionary could have such love for and patience with the pagan people among whom he had so long ministered.

Livingstone literally spent himself in untiring service for those whom he had no reason to love except for Christ's sake. Stanley wrote in his journal, "When I saw that unwearied patience, that unflagging zeal, and those enlightened sons of Africa, I became a Christian at his side, though he never spoke to me one word."

Aristotle said that the greatest Greek virtue was refusal to tolerate any insult and readiness to strike back. But that is not God's way for His people. The patient saint accepts whatever other people do to him. He is "patient with everyone" (1 Thess. 5:14), even those who try his patience to the limit. He is patient with those who slander him and who question his motives for serving the Lord.

The patient saint accepts God's plan for everything, without questioning or grumbling. He does not complain when his calling seems less glamorous than someone else's or when the Lord sends him to a place that is dangerous or difficult. He remembers that God the Son left His heavenly home of love, holiness, and glory to come to earth and be hated, rejected, spat upon, and crucified—without once returning evil for evil or complaining to His Father.

4. Forbearing Love

A fourth characteristic element of the worthy Christian walk is showing "tolerance to one another in love." Another word for tolerance is "forbearing" (see ESV, KJV, RSV). Peter tells us that such "love covers a multitude of sins" (1 Pet. 4:8). It throws a blanket over the sins of others, not to justify or excuse them but to keep the sins from becoming any more known than necessary. "Hatred stirs up strife, but love covers all transgressions" (Prov. 10:12). Such forbearing love takes abuse from others while continuing to love them.

Forbearing love could only be *agapē* love, because only *agapē* love gives continuously and unconditionally. *Erōs* love is essentially self-love, because it cares for others only because of what it can get from them. It is the love that takes and never gives. *Philia* love is primarily reciprocal love, love that gives as long as it receives. But *agapē* love is unqualified and unselfish love, love that willingly gives whether it receives in return or not. It is unconquerable benevolence, invincible goodness—love that goes out even to enemies and prays for its persecutors (Matt. 5:43–44). That is why the forbearance of which Paul speaks here could only be expressed in *agapē* love.

5. Unity

The ultimate outcome of humility, gentleness, patience, and forbearance is "being diligent to preserve the unity of the Spirit in the bond of peace" (Eph. 4:3). The Greek word for diligent, *Spoudazō,* basically means to make haste, and from that come the meanings of zeal and diligence. One commentator describes it as a holy zeal that demands full dedication. Paul used the word in telling Timothy, "Be diligent to present yourself approved to God as a workman who does not need to be ashamed, accurately handling the word of truth" (2 Tim. 2:15; cf. Titus 3:12–13).

OUR CONSTANT CONCERN: UNITY THROUGH THE HOLY SPIRIT

Preservation of the "unity of the Spirit in the bond of peace" should be the diligent and constant concern of every believer. Paul is not speaking of organizational unity, such as that promoted in many denominations and in the ecumenical movement. He is speaking of the inner and universal unity of the Spirit by which every true believer is bound to every other true believer. As Paul makes clear, this is the unity of the Spirit working in the lives of believers. It does not come from the outside but the inside, and is manifested through the inner qualities of humility, gentleness, patience, and forbearing love.

Spiritual unity is not, and cannot be, created by the church. It is already created by the Holy Spirit. "For by one Spirit we were all baptized into one body, whether Jews or Greeks, whether slaves or free, and we were all made to drink of one Spirit. . . . There are many members, but one body" (1 Cor. 12:13, 20; cf. Rom. 8:9). It is this very unity of the Spirit for which Jesus so earnestly prayed in the upper room shortly before His betrayal and arrest: "Holy Father, keep them in Your name, the name which You have given Me, that they may be one even as We are. . . . that they may all be one; even as You, Father, are in Me, and I in You, that they also may be in Us, . . . [And] the glory which You have given Me I have given to them, that they may be one, just as We are one; I in them and You in Me, that they may be perfected in unity" (John 17:11, 21–23).

OUR PART IN UNITY: WALKING IN A WORTHY MANNER

The church's responsibility, through the lives of individual believers, is to preserve unity by faithfully walking in a manner worthy of God's calling (v. 1), manifesting Christ to the world by oneness in Him (cf. Rom. 15:1–6; 1 Cor. 1:10–13; 3:1–3; Phil. 1:27). The world is always seeking but never finding unity. All the laws, conferences, treaties, accords, and agreements fail to bring unity or peace. Someone has reported that throughout recorded history every treaty made has been broken. There is not, and cannot be, any peace for the wicked (Isa. 48:22). As long as self is at the center—as long as our feelings, prestige, and rights are our chief concern—there will never be unity.

The bond that preserves unity is peace, the spiritual belt that surrounds and binds God's holy people together. It is the bond that Paul described in Philippians as "being of the same mind, maintaining the same love, united in spirit, intent on one purpose" (2:2). Behind this bond of peace is love, which Colossians 3:14 calls "the perfect bond of unity."

Humility gives birth to gentleness, gentleness gives birth to patience, patience gives birth to forbearing love, and all four of those characteristics "preserve the unity of the Spirit in the bond of peace" (Eph. 4:3). These virtues and the supernatural unity to which they testify are probably the most powerful testimony the church can have, because they are in such contrast to the attitudes and the disunity of the world. No program or method, no matter how carefully planned and executed, can open the door to the gospel in the way individual believers can do when they are genuinely humble, meek, patient, forbearing in love, and demonstrate peaceful unity in the Holy Spirit.

THE CAUSE OF THE WORTHY WALK

There is one body and one Spirit, just as also you were called in one hope of your calling; one Lord, one faith, one baptism, one God and Father of all who is over all and through all and in all. (4:4–6)

Everything that relates to salvation, the church, and the kingdom of God is based on the concept of unity, as reflected in Paul's use of seven ones in these three verses. The cause, or basis, of outward oneness is inner oneness. Practical oneness is based on spiritual oneness. To emphasize the unity of the Spirit, Paul recites the features of oneness that are germane to our doctrine and life.

Paul does not develop the particular areas of oneness, but simply lists them: body, Spirit, hope, Lord, faith, baptism, and God and Father. His focus is on the oneness of those and every other aspect of God's nature, plan, and work as a basis for our commitment to live as one. It is obvious that verse 4 centers on the Holy Spirit, verse 5 on the Son, and verse 6 on the Father.

Unity in the Spirit

There is one body and one Spirit, just as also you were called in one hope of your calling; (4:4)

There is only one body of believers, the church, which is composed of every saint who has trusted or will trust in Christ as Savior and Lord. There is no denominational, geographical, ethnic, or racial body. There is no Gentile, Jewish, male, female, slave, or freeman body. There is only Christ's body, and the unity of that body is the heart of the book of Ephesians.

Obviously there is but one Spirit, the Holy Spirit of God, who is possessed by every believer and who is therefore the inner unifying force in the body. Believers are individual temples of the Holy Spirit (1 Cor. 3:16–17) that are collectively "being fitted together [and are] growing into a holy temple in the Lord, . . . being built together into a dwelling of God in the Spirit" (Eph. 2:21–22). The Spirit "is given as a pledge of our inheritance, with a view to the redemption of God's own possession, to the praise of His glory" (Eph. 1:14). He is the divine engagement ring (pledge), as it were, who guarantees that every believer will be at the marriage supper of the Lamb (Rev. 19:9).

If all Christians were walking in obedience to and in the power of the Holy Spirit, first our doctrine and then our relationships would be purified and unified. The spiritual unity that already exists would be practically manifested in complete harmony among the people of God.

Believers are also unified in the one hope of their calling. Our calling to salvation is ultimately a calling to Christlike eternal perfection and glory. In Christ we have different gifts, different ministries, different places of service, but only one calling, to "be holy

35

and blameless before Him" (Eph. 1:4) and "to become conformed to the image of His Son" (Rom. 8:29), which will occur when we see the glorified Christ (1 John 3:2). It is the Spirit who has placed us in the one Body and who guarantees our future glory.

UNITY IN THE SON

one Lord, one faith, one baptism, (Eph. 4:5)

Just as obviously, there is but one Lord, Jesus Christ our Savior. "There is salvation in no one else; for there is no other name under heaven that has been given among men, by which we must be saved" (Acts 4:12). Paul told the Galatians, "Even if we, or an angel from heaven, should preach to you a gospel contrary to that which we have preached to you, he is to be accursed" (Gal. 1:8). "For the same Lord is Lord of all, abounding in riches for all who call on Him" (Rom. 10:12).

Consequently there can only be one faith. Paul is not referring here to the act of faith by which a person is saved or the continuing faith that produces right living, but rather the body of doctrine revealed in the New Testament. In true Christianity there is only one faith, "the faith which was once for all handed down to the saints" and for which we are to contend (Jude 3). Our one faith is the content of the revealed Word of God. Lack of faithful and careful study of His Word, unexamined tradition, worldly influences, carnal inclinations, and many other things fragment doctrine into many varying and even contradictory forms. God's Word contains many truths, but its individual truths are but harmonious facets of His one truth, which is our one faith.

There is but one baptism among believers. Spiritual baptism, by which all believers are placed into the Body by the Holy Spirit, is implied in verse 4. The "one baptism" of verse 5 is best taken to refer to water baptism, the common New Testament means of a believer's publicly confessing Jesus as Savior and Lord. This is preferred because of the way Paul has spoken specifically of each member of the Trinity in succession. This is the Lord Jesus Christ's verse, as it were.

Water baptism was extremely important in the early church, not as a means of salvation or special blessing but as a testimony of identity with and unity in Jesus Christ. Believers were not baptized in the name of a local church, a prominent evangelist, a leading elder, or even an apostle, but only in the name of Christ (see 1 Cor. 1:13–17). Those who by one Lord are in one faith testify to that unity in one baptism.

Unity in the Father

one God and Father of all who is over all and through all and in all. (4:6)

The basic doctrine of Judaism has always been, "The Lord is our God, the Lord is one!" (Deut. 6:4; see also 4:35; 32:39; Isa. 45:14; 46:9), and God's oneness is just as foundational to Christianity (see 1 Cor. 8:4–6; Eph. 4:3–6; James 2:19). Yet the New Testament also reveals the more complete truth that the one God is in three Persons—Father, Son, and Holy Spirit (Matt. 28:19; John 6:27; 20:28; Acts 5:3–4).

God the Father is often used in Scripture as the most comprehensive and inclusive divine title, though it is clear from many New Testament texts that He is never separated in nature or power from the Son or the Holy Spirit. Paul's point here is not to separate the Persons of the Godhead but to note their unique roles and yet focus on their unity in relation to each other and in relation to the church—manifested in the several different aspects mentioned in these three verses.

Our "one God and Father," along with the Son and the Holy Spirit, is "over all and through all and in all." That comprehensive statement points to the glorious, divine, eternal unity that the Father gives believers by His Spirit and through the Son. We are God created, God loved, God saved, God Fathered, God controlled, God sustained, God filled, and God blessed. We are one people under one sovereign ("over all"), omnipotent ("through all"), and omnipresent ("in all") God.

Chapter 2

WALKING AS
A NEW PERSON

EPHESIANS 4:17–24

So this I say, and affirm together with the Lord, that you walk no longer just as the Gentiles also walk, in the futility of their mind, being darkened in their understanding, excluded from the life of God because of the ignorance that is in them, because of the hardness of their heart; and they, having become callous, have given themselves over to sensuality for the practice of every kind of impurity with greediness. But you did not learn Christ in this way, if indeed you have heard Him and have been taught in Him, just as truth is in Jesus, that, in reference to your former manner of life, you lay aside the old self, which is being corrupted in accordance with the lusts of deceit, and that you be renewed in the spirit of your mind, and put on the new self, which in the likeness of God has been created in righteousness and holiness of the truth. (4:17–24)

When a person believes and confesses Jesus Christ as Lord and is thereby born again, a transformation takes place in his or her basic nature. The change is even more radical than the change that will take place at death.

When a believer dies, he has already been fitted for heaven, already been made a citizen of the kingdom, already become a child of God. He simply begins to perfectly experience the divine nature he has had since his spiritual birth, because for the first time he is free from the unredeemed flesh. The future receiving of his glorified body (cf. 1 Cor. 15:42–54) will not make him better, since he is already perfected; but it will give him the full capacity for all that eternal resurrection life involves.

Salvation is not a matter of improvement or perfection of what has previously existed. It is total transformation. The New Testament speaks of believers having a new mind, a new will, a new heart, a new inheritance, a new relationship, new power, new knowledge, new wisdom, new perception, and a new understanding. They also have a new righteousness, a new love, new desire, new citizenship, and many other new things—all of these possessions are summed up as "newness of life" (Rom. 6:4).

At the new birth a person becomes a "new creature; the old things passed away; behold, new things have come" (2 Cor. 5:17). It is not simply that he receives something new but that he *becomes* someone new. "I have been crucified with Christ," Paul said; "and it is no longer I who live, but Christ lives in me; and the life which I now live in the flesh I live by faith in the Son of God, who loved me and gave Himself up for me" (Gal. 2:20). The new nature is not added to the old nature but replaces it. The transformed person is a completely new "I." In contrast to the former love of evil (cf. John 3:19–21; Rom. 1:21–25; 28–32), that new self—the deepest, truest part of the Christian—now loves the law of God, longs to fulfill its righteous demands, hates sin, and longs for deliverance from the unredeemed flesh, which houses his eternal new creation until the day of glorification (see Rom. 7:14–25; 8:22–24).

Why, then, do we continue to sin after we become Christians? As Paul explains in Romans 7, "No longer am I the one doing it, but sin which dwells in me. For I know that nothing good dwells in me, that is, in my flesh; for the willing is present in me, but the doing of the good is not" (vv. 17–18; cf. 20). Sin still resides in our flesh, so that we are inhibited and restrained from being able to give full and perfect expression to the new nature. Possessing the fullness of the divine nature without the corruption of our unredeemed flesh is a promise we will realize only in the future (cf. Rom. 8:23; Phil. 3:20–21; 2 Pet. 1:3–4).

Biblical terminology, then, does not say that a Christian has two different natures. He has but one nature, the new nature in Christ. The old self dies and the new self lives; they do not coexist. It is not a remaining old nature but the remaining garment of sinful flesh that causes Christians to sin. The Christian is a single new person, a totally new creation, not a spiritual schizophrenic. It is the filthy coat of remaining humanness in which the new creation dwells that continues to hinder and contaminate his living. The believer as a total person is transformed but not yet wholly perfect. He has residing sin but no longer reigning sin (cf. Rom. 6:14). He is no longer the old man corrupted but is now the new man created in righteousness and holiness, awaiting full salvation (cf. Rom. 13:11).

In Ephesians 4 Paul makes two appeals based on the fact that believers are new creations. The first begins the chapter: "I, therefore, . . . implore you to walk in a manner worthy of the calling with which you have been called" (v. 1). The second (v. 17) introduces the present text, in which Paul contrasts the walk of the wicked unbeliever with the walk of the spiritual Christian. He follows that contrast with more "therefores" (v. 25; 5:1, 7, 15), showing the Christian's proper response to being a new creation. All of this points to the fact that a changed nature demands changed behavior. It is as if the apostle is saying, "Since God has created a marvelous new entity in the world called the church, and because of this unique creation—with its unique character of humility, its unique empowerment with spiritual gifts, its unique unity as the Body of Christ, and its need to be built up in love—here is how every believer should live as a member of that church."

In verses 17–24, Paul moves from the general to the specific, first giving four characteristics of the walk of the old man and then four characteristics of the walk of the new.

THE WALK OF THE OLD SELF

So this I say and affirm together with the Lord, that you walk no longer just as the Gentiles also walk, in the futility of their mind, being darkened in their understanding, excluded from the life of God because of the ignorance that is in them, because of the hardness of their heart; and they, having become callous, have given themselves over to sensuality for the practice of every kind of impurity with greediness. (4:17–19)

Because we are called to salvation, unified in the Body of Christ, gifted by the Holy Spirit, and built up by the gifted men (vv. 1–16), we should "walk no longer just as the Gentiles also walk." We cannot accomplish the glorious work of Christ by continuing to live the way the world lives.

The Greek word *ethnos* ("Gentiles") in verse 17 basically refers to a multitude of people in general, and then to a group of people of a particular kind. It is this secondary meaning that we see in our derived English word *ethnic*. Jews used the term in two common ways, first to distinguish all other people from Jews and second to distinguish all religions from Judaism. Gentiles therefore referred racially and ethnically to all non-Jews and religiously to all pagans.

In his first letter to the Thessalonians Paul uses the term in its pagan meaning when he refers to "the Gentiles who do not know God" (1 Thess. 4:5), and that is the sense in which he uses it in our present text. "Gentiles" here represent all ungodly, unregenerate, pagan persons.

Like the church in our own day, the churches at Ephesus and in almost every non-Palestinian area in New Testament times were surrounded by rank paganism and its attendant immorality. Ephesus was a leading commercial and cultural city of the Roman Empire. It boasted the great pagan temple of Artemis, or Diana, one of the seven wonders of the ancient world. But it was also a leading city in debauchery and sexual immorality. Some historians rank it as the most lascivious city of Asia Minor.

The temple of Artemis was the center of much of the wickedness. Like those in most pagan religions, its rituals and practices were but extensions of man's vilest and most perverted sins. Male and female roles were interchanged, and orgiastic sex, homosexuality, and every other sexual perversion were common. Artemis was herself a sex goddess, represented by an ugly, repulsive female idol that looked something like a cross between a cow and a wolf. She was served by thousands of temple prostitutes, eunuchs, singers, dancers, and priests and priestesses. Idols of Artemis and other deities were to be seen everywhere, in every size and made out of many different materials. Of special popularity were silver idols and religious artifacts. It was because Paul's preaching cut deeply into that trade that the Ephesian silversmiths rallied the populace against him and his fellow believers (Acts 19:24–28).

The temple of Artemis contained one of the richest art

collections then in existence. It was also used as a bank, because most people feared stealing from within its walls lest they incur the wrath of the goddess or other deities. A quarter-mile-wide perimeter served as an asylum for criminals, who were safe from apprehension and punishment as long as they remained within the temple confines. For obvious reasons, the presence of hundreds of hardened criminals added still further to Ephesus's corruption and vice. The fifth-century B.C. Greek philosopher Heraclitus, himself a pagan, referred to Ephesus as "the darkness of vileness. The morals were lower than animals and the inhabitants of Ephesus were fit only to be drowned." There is no reason to believe that the situation had changed much by Paul's day. If anything, it may have been worse.

The church at Ephesus was a small island of despised people in a giant cesspool of wickedness. Most of the believers had themselves once been a part of that paganism. They frequently passed by places where they once caroused and ran into friends with whom they once indulged in debauchery. They faced continual temptations to revert to the old ways, and the apostle therefore admonished them to resist. "This I say therefore, and affirm together with the Lord, that you walk no longer just as the Gentiles walk." Peter gave a similar word when he wrote, "For the time already past is sufficient for you to have carried out the desire of the Gentiles, having pursued a course of sensuality, lusts, drunkenness, carousing, drinking parties and abominable idolatries. In all this, they are surprised that you do not run with them into the same excesses of dissipation, and they malign you" (1 Peter 4:3–4).

On the basis of what we are in Christ and of all that God now purposes for us as His redeemed and beloved children, we are to be absolutely distinct from the rest of the world, which does not know or follow Him. Spiritually we have already left the world and are now citizens of heaven. We are therefore not to "love the world nor the things in the world. If anyone loves the world, the love of the Father is not in him. For all that is in the world, the lust of the flesh and the lust of the eyes and the boastful pride of life, is not from the Father, but is from the world. The world is passing away, and also its lusts; but the one who does the will of God lives forever" (1 John 2:15–17). The world's standards are wrong, its motives are wrong, its aims are wrong. Its ways are sinful, deceitful, corrupt, empty, and destructive.

The warning Paul gives did not originate from his own personal tastes or preferences; he writes, "This I say . . . and affirm together with the Lord." The matter of forsaking sin and following righteousness is not the whim of isolated, narrow-minded preachers and teachers. It is God's own standard and His only standard for those who belong to Him. It is the very essence of the gospel and is set in bold contrast to the standards of the unredeemed.

Characteristics of the Old Self

Paul proceeds to give four specific characteristics of the ungodly, pagan lifestyle that believers are to forsake. The worldly life is intellectually futile, ignorant of God's truth, spiritually and morally callous, and depraved in mind.

1. Intellectually Futile

The first characteristic of unregenerate people is that they live "in the futility of their mind." It is significant that the basic issue of lifestyle centers in the mind. Paul continues to speak of understanding and ignorance (v. 18), learning and teaching (vv. 20–21), and the mind and truth (vv. 23–24)—all of which are related to the intellect. Because unbelievers and Christians *think* differently they are therefore to *act* differently. As far as spiritual and moral issues are concerned, an unbeliever cannot think straight. His rational processes in those areas are warped and inadequate (cf. Rom. 1:28; 8:7; 1 Cor. 2:14; Col. 2:18; Titus 1:15).

Because man's sinfulness flows out of his reprobate mind, the transformation must begin with the mind (v. 23). Christianity is cognitive before it is experiential. It is our thinking that makes us consider the gospel and our thinking that causes us to believe the historic facts and spiritual truths of the gospel and to receive Christ as Lord and Savior. That is why the first step in repentance is a change of mind about oneself, about one's spiritual condition, and about God.

To the Greeks the mind was all-important. They prided themselves in their great literature, art, philosophy, politics, and science. They were so advanced in their learning that Greek slaves were prized by the Romans and other conquerors as tutors for their children and as managers of their households and businesses. Greeks believed that almost any problem could be reasoned to a solution.

Yet Paul says that spiritually the operation of the natural mind is futile and unproductive. The Greek word *mataiotēs* ("futility" in verse 17) refers to that which fails to produce the desired result, that which never succeeds. It was therefore used as a synonym for empty, because it amounts to nothing. The spiritual thinking and resulting lifestyle of "the Gentiles"—here representing all the ungodly—is inevitably empty, vain, and void of substance. The life of an unbeliever is bound up in thinking and acting in an arena of ultimate trivia. He consumes himself in the pursuit of goals that are purely selfish, in the accumulation of that which is temporary, and in looking for satisfaction in that which is intrinsically deceptive and disappointing.

The unregenerate person plans and resolves everything on the basis of his own thinking. He becomes his own ultimate authority and he follows his own thinking to its ultimate outcome of futility, aimlessness, and meaninglessness—to the self-centered emptiness that characterizes our age (cf. Ps. 94:8–11; Acts 14:15; Rom. 1:21–22).

After a life of experiencing every worldly advantage and pleasure, the wisest, wealthiest, and most favored man of the ancient world concluded that the worldly life is "vanity and striving after wind" (Eccles. 2:26; cf. 1:2; 14; 2:11; etc.). Yet century after century, millennium after millennium, men and women go on seeking the same futile goals in the same futile ways.

2. Ignorant of God's Truth

The second characteristic of ungodly persons is ignorance of God's truth. Their thinking not only is futile but spiritually uninformed. They are "darkened in their understanding, excluded from the life of God, because of the ignorance that is in them, because of the hardness of their heart."

General education and higher learning are more accessible today than ever. College graduates number in the tens of millions, and our society, like ancient Greece, prides itself in its science, technology, literature, art, and other achievements of the mind. For many people, to be called ignorant is a greater offense than to be called sinful. Yet Paul's point in this passage is that ignorance and sin are inseparable. The ungodly may be "always learning," but they are "never able to come to the knowledge of the truth" (2 Tim. 3:7). Fallen mankind has a built-in inability to know and comprehend the things of God—the only things that ultimately are worth knowing. When men rejected God, "they became futile in their speculations, and their foolish heart was darkened" (Rom. 1:21). Intellectual futility and foolishness combine as part of sin's penalty.

The Greek word behind "being darkened" is a perfect participle, indicating a continuing condition of spiritual darkness. This darkness implies both ignorance and immorality. And darkness "of their understanding" is coupled with exclusion "from the life of God" (cf. John 1:5). The cause of their darkness, ignorance, and separation from God is "the hardness of their heart," their willful determination to remain in sin. Because men determine to reject Him, God judicially and sovereignly determines to blind their minds, exclude them from His presence, and confirm them in their spiritual ignorance. "For even though they knew God, they did not honor Him as God or give thanks," Paul explains of fallen mankind. "Professing to be wise, they became fools, . . . Therefore God gave them over in the lusts of their hearts to impurity" (Rom. 1:21–22, 24).

"Because of the hardness of their heart" (Eph. 4:18), the ungodly are unresponsive to truth (cf. Isa. 44:18–20; 1 Thess. 4:5). Just as a corpse cannot hear a conversation in the mortuary, the person who is spiritually "dead in [his] trespasses and sins" (Eph. 2:1) cannot hear or understand the things of God, no matter how loudly or clearly they may be declared or evidenced in his presence. *Pōrōsis* ("hardness") carries the idea of being rock hard. It was used by physicians to describe the calcification that forms around broken bones and becomes harder than the bone itself. It was also used of the hard formations that sometimes occur in joints and cause them to become immobile. It could therefore connote the idea of paralysis as well as of hardness. Sin has a petrifying effect, and the heart of the person who continually chooses to sin becomes hardened and paralyzed to spiritual truth, utterly insensitive to the things of God.

Satan plays a part in the blindness of those who refuse to believe, because "the god of this world has blinded the minds of the unbelieving so that they might not see the light of the gospel of the glory of Christ, who is the image of God" (2 Cor. 4:4). They refuse to see Christ because they refuse to see God, and their refusal is readily confirmed and reinforced by the god of this world.

And when men continually persist in following their own way, they will also eventually be confirmed in their choice by the God of heaven. The Jews who heard Jesus teach and preach had the great advantage of having had God's Word given to them through Moses, the prophets, and other Old Testament writers. They had the even greater advantage of seeing and hearing God's own incarnate Son. But "though He had performed so many signs before them," John tells us, "yet they were not believing in Him. . . . For this reason they could not believe, for Isaiah said again, 'He has blinded their eyes and He hardened their heart, so that they would not see with their eyes and perceive with their heart, and be converted and I heal them'" (John 12:37, 39–40). Because they would not believe, they could not believe. God one day says, "Let the one who does wrong, still do wrong; and let the one who is filthy, still be filthy" (Rev. 22:11).

When men choose to petrify their hearts by constant rejection of the light (John 12:35–36), they became "darkened in their understanding, excluded from the life of God, because of the ignorance that is in them, because of the hardness of their heart" (Eph. 4:18). That is the unspeakable tragedy of unbelief, the tragedy of the person who makes himself his own god.

3. Spiritually and Morally Calloused

The third characteristic of the unregenerate person is spiritual and moral callousness—"they . . . become callous." When people continue in sin and turn themselves away from the life of God, they become apathetic and insensitive about moral and spiritual things. They reject all standards of righteousness and do not care about the consequences of their unrighteous thoughts and actions. Even conscience becomes scarred with tissue that is not sensitive to wrong (1 Tim. 4:2; Titus 1:15).

According to an ancient Greek story, a Spartan youth stole a fox but then inadvertently came upon the man from whom he had stolen it. To keep his theft from being discovered, the boy stuck the fox inside his clothes and stood without moving a muscle while the frightened fox tore out his vital organs. Even at the cost of his own painful death he would not own up to his wrong.

Our wicked society is so determined not to be discovered for what it is that it stands unflinching as its very life and vitality is ripped apart by the sins and corruption it holds so dear. It has become callous both to the reality and to the consequences of sin, and will endure any agony rather than admit that its way of "living" is the way of death.

On the other hand, sins that were once hidden or excused are now indulged in openly and blatantly. Often not even the semblance of morality is maintained. When self-desire rules, indecency runs wild and proceeds to cauterize the conscience, the God-given warning light and pain center of the soul. Those who are dying are desensitized to that which is killing them—because they choose it that way. Even when held up shamefully in full view of the world, their sins are not recognized as sinful or as the cause of increasing meaninglessness, hopelessness, and despair (cf. Rom. 1:32).

4. Depraved in Mind

Futile, self-centered thinking, ignorance of the truth, and spiritual and moral callousness lead inevitably "to sensuality, for the practice of every kind of impurity with greediness." Such sensuality characterizes the fourth characteristic of the unregenerate person, a depraved mind.

Aselgeia (sensuality) refers to total licentiousness, the absence of all moral restraint, especially in the area of sexual sins. One commentator says the term relates to "a disposition of the soul incapable of bearing the pain of discipline." The idea is that of unbridled self-indulgence and undisciplined obscenity.

Sensuality characterizes the people Peter describes as "those who indulge the flesh in its corrupt desires and despise authority. Daring, self-willed, they do not tremble when they revile angelic majesties, whereas angels who are greater in might and power do not bring a reviling judgment against them before the Lord. But these, like unreasoning animals, born as creatures of instinct to be captured and killed, reviling where they have no knowledge, will in the destruction of those creatures also be destroyed" (2 Peter 2:10–12).

All people initially recognize at least some standard of right and wrong and have a certain sense of shame when they act against that standard. Consequently, they usually try to hide their wrongdoing. They may continually fall back into it but still recognize it as wrong, as something they should not be doing; and conscience will not let them remain comfortable. But as they continue to overrule their conscience and train themselves to do evil and to ignore guilt, they eventually reject those standards and determine to live solely by their own desires, thereby revealing an already seared conscience. Having rejected all divine guidelines and protection, they become *depraved in mind* and give themselves over to sensuality. Such a person cares nothing about what other people think—not to mention about what God thinks—but only about what gratifies the cravings of his own warped mind.

Ungodliness and its attendant immorality destroy the mind as well as the conscience and the spirit. Rejection of God and of His truth and righteousness finally results in what Paul refers to in Romans as a "depraved mind" (1:28)—a mind that is no mind, that cannot reason, that cannot think clearly, that cannot recognize or understand God's truth, and that loses contact with spiritual reality. In its extreme, the depraved mind loses contact with *all* reality. That is the mindlessness of the self-indulgent, profligate celebrity who loses his career, his sanity, and often his life because of wanton sensuality. When indecency becomes a way of life, every aspect of life is corrupted, distorted, and eventually destroyed.

The rapid increase in some forms of mental illness today can be laid largely at the feet of increased sensuality of every sort. Man is made for God and designed according to His standards. When he rejects God and His standards he destroys himself in the process. The corruptions of our present society are not the result of psychological or sociological circumstances but the result of personal choices based on principles that are specifically and purposely against God and His way. Homosexuality, sexual perversion, abortion, lying, cheating, stealing, murder, and every other type of moral degeneration have become unabashed and calloused ways of life through the conscious choices of those who indulge in them.

Ergasia, the Greek word translated "practice," can refer to a business enterprise, and that idea could apply here. The ungodly person often makes business out of "every kind of impurity." Some years ago a Christian leader commented bluntly that many of the books published in the United States today rival the drippings of a broken sewer. Yet pornography, prostitution, X-rated films, provocative TV programs, and every kind of impurity form perhaps the largest industry in America. The vast majority of it is open, unashamed, and legally protected.

An article in *Forbes* magazine a few decades ago, entitled "The X-Rated Economy,"[1] began by stating the obvious: pornography is no longer an illegal business. The market for pornography is not confined to perverts and criminal elements. To the contrary, the largest part of the market is middle-class people. In an increasingly permissive society, those looking for pornography are free to revel in it. The surprising revelation was that the nation's pornographers do billions of dollars worth of business a year—more than the combined incomes of the often supportive movie and music industries! As we approach the year 2020, high-definition picture quality and video streaming offer provocative and often graphic images for home TV and computer screens. And without Internet filters, it is easy for anyone to view, even unintentionally, inappropriate websites. Such impurity is available on PCs, smartphones, and any electronic device that can access the Worldwide Web.

Impurity is inseparable from greediness. *Pleonexia,* the Greek word for greediness at the end of verse 19, means unbounded covetousness, uninhibited lust for that which is wanted. Immorality has no part in love, and anything the sensual person does under the guise of caring and helpfulness is but a ruse for exploitation. The world of sensuality and impurity is part of the world of greediness. The person given over to godlessness and immorality greedily takes whatever he can from those around him. He evaluates life only in material terms (Luke 12:15), uses other people to his own advantage (1 Thess. 2:5; 2 Pet. 2:3), and turns his back on God in order to fulfill his own evil desires (Rom. 1:29). And his greediness is no less than idolatry (Col. 3:5).

When a person determines to think his own way, do things his own way, and pursue his own destiny, he cuts himself off from God. When that happens, he cuts himself off from truth and becomes spiritually blind and without standards of morality. Without standards of morality, immorality becomes a shameless and calloused way of life. When that is continued it destroys the mind's ability to distinguish good from evil, truth from falsehood, and reality from unreality. The godless life becomes the mindless life.

That process characterizes every unbeliever. It is the direction that every ungodly person is headed, although some are further along than others. "Evil men and impostors will proceed from bad to worse, deceiving and being deceived" (2 Tim. 3:13). That some people may not reach the extremes Paul mentions in Ephesians 4:17–19 is due only to the protective shield of God's common grace that He showers both on the righteous and the unrighteous (see Matt. 5:45) and to the preserving influence of the Holy Spirit (Job 34:14–15) and of the church (Matt. 5:13).

The Walk of the New Self

But you did not learn Christ in this way, if indeed you have heard Him and have been taught in Him, just as truth is in Jesus, that, in reference to your former manner of life, you lay aside the old self, which is being corrupted in accordance with the lusts of deceit, and that you be renewed in the spirit of your mind, and put on the new self, which in the likeness of God has been created in righteousness and holiness of the truth. (4:20–24)

The new walk in Christ is the exact opposite of the old walk of the flesh. Whereas the old is self-centered and futile, the new is Christ-centered and purposeful. Whereas the old is ignorant of God's truth, the new knows and understands it. Whereas the old is morally and spiritually calloused and shameless, the new is sensitive to sin of every sort. Whereas the old is depraved in its thinking, the new is renewed.

Christ-centered

But you did not learn Christ in this way, (4:20)

After reviewing the evils of the pagan world and the self-centered, purposeless wickedness that both comes from and leads to spiritual darkness and ignorance, Paul declared to believers who had fallen back into such degradation, "But you did not learn Christ in this way." That is not the way of Christ or of His kingdom or family. In effect, Paul wrote, "You are not to have any part of such things, whether by participation or association."

"You did not learn Christ" is a direct reference to salvation. To learn Christ is to be saved. While it is true that the verb *manthanō* can be used in reference to the process of learning truth (see Rom. 16:17; Phil. 4:9), it can also mean "to come to know,"[2] as a one-time act, particularly when the verb is aorist active indicative, as in this case. The aorist is also used in John 6:45, where Jesus spoke to those who had "learned from the Father"—indicating a reference to the saving act of faith under the old covenant, which would lead them now to Him.

In Matthew 11:29, Jesus offered one of the loveliest of all salvation invitations: "Take my yoke upon you, and learn of me" (KJV). This use of *manthanō* is also in the aorist tense, indicating a single unrepeated act. Both the context and the use of the aorist tense of the verb "to learn" in these passages lead to the conclusion that this learning refers to the moment of saving faith.

"Friendship with the world is hostility toward God," James wrote (4:4), and the person who makes a profession of Christ but makes no effort to break with his worldly and sinful habits has reason to doubt his salvation. "The one who says, 'I have come to know Him,' and does not keep His commandments, is a liar, and the truth is not in him," and "If anyone loves the world, the love of the Father is not in him" (1 John 2:4, 15).

The ways of God and the ways of the world are not compatible. The idea, promoted by some who claim to be evangelicals, that a Christian does not have to give up anything or change anything when he becomes a Christian is nothing less than diabolical. That notion, under the pretense of elevating God's grace and of protecting the gospel from works righteousness, will do nothing but send many people confidently down the broad way that Jesus said leads to destruction (Matt. 7:13).

From the human side, salvation begins with repentance, a change of mind and action regarding sin, self, and God. John the Baptist (Matt. 3:2), Jesus (Matt. 4:17), and the apostles (Acts 2:38; 3:19; 5:31; 20:21; 26:20) began their ministries with the preaching of repentance. The very purpose of receiving Christ is to "be saved from this perverse generation" (Acts 2:40), and no one is saved who does not repent and forsake sin. Although no Christian is totally free from the presence of sin in this life, in Christ he is willingly freed from his orientation to sin. Believers may slip and fall many times, but the determined direction of their lives will be *away from* sin.

One of the first things a Christian should learn is that he or she cannot trust their own thinking or rely on their own way. "They who live might no longer live for themselves, but for Him who died and rose again on their behalf" (2 Cor. 5:15). Every Christian has the mind of Christ (1 Cor. 2:16), and Christ's is the only mind on which they can rely. The obedient, faithful Christian is the one for whom Christ thinks, acts, loves, feels, serves, and lives in every way. The believer says with Paul, "I have been crucified with Christ; and it is no longer I who live, but Christ lives in me; and the life which I now live in the flesh I live by faith in the Son of God, who loved me, and gave Himself up for me" (Gal. 2:20).

Because we have the mind of Christ, we are to "have this attitude in [ourselves] which was also in Christ Jesus," who "humbled Himself by becoming obedient to the point of death, even death on a cross" (Phil. 2:5, 8). Although Christ was one with His Father, while on earth He did absolutely nothing but His Father's will (Matt. 26:39, 42; John 4:34; 5:30; 6:38; etc.). If the incarnate Lord sought the mind of His heavenly Father in everything He did, how much more should we? The mark of the Christian life is to think like Christ, act like Christ, love like Christ, and in every possible way to be like Christ—in order that "whether we are awake or asleep, we will live together with Him" (1 Thess. 5:10).

God has a plan of destiny for the universe, and as long as Christ is working in us He is working out a part of that plan through us. The Christ-centered life is the most purposeful and meaningful life conceivable—it is part of the divine plan and work of God!

Knows God's Truth

if indeed you have heard Him and have been taught in Him, just as truth is in Jesus, (4:21)

Instead of being ignorant of God's truth, the Christian has heard Christ and is taught in Him. Both verbs are in the aorist tense, again pointing to a one-time past act, and in this context referring to the time when the readers were taught and came to believe the gospel—here called the "truth . . . in Jesus." These terms describe the moment of salvation: conversion. When a person receives Christ as Savior and Lord, he comes into God's truth.

"If indeed you have heard Him and have been taught in Him" (cf. Matt. 17:5) could not possibly refer to hearing Jesus' physical voice on earth, because there is no way that could have been true of all the believers in Asia Minor to whom Paul was writing. It must refer to the hearing of His spiritual call to salvation (cf. John 8:47; 10:27; Acts 3:22–23; Heb. 3:7–8). Many New Testament references speak of this hearing and being taught as the call of God (e.g., Acts 2:39). *En autoi* ("in Him") means in union with Christ and further emphasizes the fact that at conversion we received the truth embodied in Christ, because we came to be in Him.

Life without God leads to cynicism about truth. The ungodly person may ask rhetorically with Pilate, "What is truth?" (John 18:38), but he expects no satisfactory answer. The Christian, however, can say, "The truth of Christ is in me" (2 Cor. 11:10).

The truth that is in Jesus Christ, then, is first of all the truth about salvation. This idea is parallel to Ephesians 1:13, where Paul says hearing the truth and being in Him are synonymous with conversion: "In Him, you also, after listening to the message of truth, the gospel of your salvation—having also believed, you were sealed in Him with the Holy Spirit of promise." The "truth . . . is in Jesus," and it leads to the fullness of truth about God, man, creation, history, sin, righteousness, grace, faith, salvation, life, death, purpose, meaning, relationships, heaven, hell, judgment, eternity—and everything else of ultimate consequence.

John summed up this relationship with truth when he wrote: "And we know that the Son of God has come, and has given us understanding so that we may know Him who is true; and we are in Him who is true, in His Son Jesus Christ. This is the true God and eternal life" (1 John 5:20).

Delivered from the Old Self

that, in reference to your former manner of life, you lay aside the old self, which is being corrupted in accordance with the lusts of deceit, (4:22)

To demonstrate the transforming nature of regeneration, the apostle further describes and defines the inherent realities of the truth in Jesus that his readers heard and were taught at conversion. He uses three infinitives (in the original Greek) to summarize what they heard in the call of the gospel: "lay aside," "be renewed" (v. 23), and "put on" (v. 24).

It is important to note that Paul is not here exhorting believers to do these things. These three infinitives describe the saving truth in Jesus and are not imperatives directed to Christians. They are done at the point of conversion, and are mentioned here only as a reminder of the reality of that experience.

"Lay aside the old self" is related to "have heard ... and have been taught" in the gospel (v. 21). Although it is essential to affirm that salvation is a divine and sovereign miracle apart from any human contribution, it also must be affirmed that men and women do hear and believe and lay aside the old while putting on the new. The saving act of God effects such responses in the believing soul.

These are not human works required for divine salvation but inherent elements of the divine work of salvation. Paul's terms here are basically a description of repentance from sin and submission to God, so often taught as elements of regeneration (see Isa. 55:6–7; Matt. 19:16–22; Acts 2:38–40; 20:21; 1 Thess. 1:9; et al.).

In contrast to the unregenerate person who continually resists and rejects God and lives in the sphere of dominating sin ("the former manner of life"), the Christian has heard the call to "lay aside the old self." The verb means to strip off, as in the case of old filthy clothes. The tense (aorist middle) indicates a once-and-forever action done by the believer at salvation.

Paul's reference to "the old self" (old in the sense of worn out and useless) is consistent with gospel terminology in his other epistles. For example, Colossians 3 describes the act of salvation using four verbs: "for you *have died* and your life is hidden with Christ in God" (v. 3); "*you have been raised up*" (v. 1); "*you laid aside* the old self [man]" (v. 9); and you "*have put on* the new self [man] who is being renewed to a true knowledge according to the image of the One who created him" (v. 10; all emphasis added). All four verbs are in the aorist tense in the Greek, indicating that they refer back to already completed action and must therefore refer to the same past event of salvation. In the context, "laid aside" and "have put on" cannot be other than exact parallels to "have died" and "have been raised up," which are clearly salvific in content.

Affirming the truth of these four aspects of conversion is the basis for the exhortations in the Colossian passage. Paul is describing salvation to the Colossians exactly as he does to the Ephesians. Although in Ephesians he does not refer specifically to the believer's union in the death and resurrection of Christ, he does allude to that reality when saying that the one who believes is "in Him."

His references to the old self and the new self in both passages are obviously parallel.

This perspective is further proved by Paul's teaching in Romans 6, where he describes the nature of salvation, with emphasis on verbs: "we . . . *died to sin*" (v. 2); "all of us . . . *have been baptized* into Christ Jesus" (v. 3); "*have been buried* with Him . . . into death" (v. 4); "*we have become united* with Him in . . . His death" (v. 5); "our old self *was crucified* with Him" (v. 6); "our body of sin *might be done away* with" (v. 6); "he who has *died*" (v. 7); and "we *have died* with Christ" (v. 8; emphasis added). Eight of those nine verbs are aorist in the Greek, looking back at an already accomplished event. One is in the perfect tense (v. 5), seeing the result of that past event. Again, Paul gives his exhortation on the basis of this description of the complete transformation of the believer at conversion (cf. Rom. 6:12–23).

The inescapable conclusion from what Paul says in Romans and Colossians is that salvation is a spiritual union with Jesus Christ in His death and resurrection that can also be described as the death of the "old self" and the resurrection of the "new self," who now walks in "newness of life." This union and new identity clearly means that salvation is transformation. It is not the addition of a new self to an old self. In Christ, the old self no longer exists (cf. 2 Cor. 5:17). That is what the Ephesians heard and were taught according to the truth in Jesus (4:21). The old self is the unconverted nature, described as "being corrupted in accordance with the lusts of deceit." The old self of the unbeliever not only is corrupt but is increasingly being corrupted (present passive), because it is the tool for evil desire which is controlled by deceit (cf. 2:1–3). The gospel invitation is to lay the old self aside in repentance from sin that includes not just sorrow about sin but a turning from sin to God.

Becomes the New Self

and that you be renewed in the spirit of your mind, and put on the new self, which in the likeness of God has been created in righteousness and holiness of the truth. (4:23–24)

In contrast to the depraved, reprobate mind of the unregenerate person (vv. 17–18), the Christian is renewed continually "in the spirit of [his] mind" (cf. Col. 3:10). *Ananeoē* (to be renewed) appears only here in the New Testament. The best rendering of this present passive infinitive is as a modifier of the main verb "put on," so that it would read "and being renewed in the spirit of your mind, put on the new self." This makes clear that such renewal is the consequence of "laying aside the old self" and is the context in which one may "put on the new self." Salvation relates to the mind, which is the center of thought, understanding, and belief, as well as of motive and action. The "spirit of your mind" is explained by one commentator as intending to show that it is not in the sphere of human thinking or human reason, but in the moral sphere, that this renewal occurs. John Eadie says:

> The change is not in the mind psychologically, either in its essence or in its operation; and neither is it in the mind as if it were a superficial change of opinion on points of doctrine or practice; but it is in the spirit of the mind; in that which gives mind both its bent and its material of thought. It is not simply in the spirit as if it lay there in dim and mystic quietude; but it is in the spirit of the mind; in the power which, when changed itself, radically alters the entire sphere and business of the inner mechanism.[3]

When a person becomes a Christian, God initially renews his mind, giving it a completely new spiritual and moral capability—a capability that the most brilliant and educated mind apart from Christ can never achieve (cf. 1 Cor. 2:9–16). This renewal continues through the believer's life as he is obedient to the Word and will of God (cf. Rom. 12:1–2). The process is not a one-time accomplishment but the continual work of the Spirit in the child of God (Titus 3:5). Our resources are God's Word and prayer. It is through these means that we gain the mind of Christ (cf. Phil. 2:5; Col. 3:16; 2 Tim. 1:7), and it is through that mind that we live the life of Christ.

The renewed spirit of the believer's mind is a corollary to putting on the new self, which is the new creation made in the very "likeness of God [and] has been created in righteousness and holiness of the truth." That which was once darkened, ignorant, hardened, calloused, sensual, impure, and greedy is now enlightened, learned in the truth, sensitive to sin, pure, and generous. Whereas it was once characterized by wickedness and sin, it is now characterized by righteousness and holiness. In Colossians 3:12, Paul calls believers the "chosen of God, holy and beloved."

It is essential to expand the concept of the new self so that it may be understood more fully. The word "new" (Gk. *kainos*) does not mean renovated but entirely new—new in species or character. The new self is new because it "has been created in the likeness of God." The Greek is literally, "according to what God is"—a staggering statement expressing the wondrous reality of salvation. Those who confess Jesus Christ as Lord are made like God! Peter says we become "partakers of the divine nature" (2 Pet. 1:4).

In Galatians 2:20, Paul declares, "It is no longer I who live, but

Christ lives in me." The image of God, lost in Adam, is more gloriously restored in the second Adam, the One who is the image of the invisible God (cf. 2 Cor. 4:4–6, where Paul describes Christ as the image of God, the treasure that dwells in us.)

If believers have received the divine nature—the life of Christ, the likeness of God in this new self by an act of divine creation (cf. Col. 3:10)—it obviously must have "been created in righteousness and holiness of the truth" (Eph. 4:24). In the Greek, the word truth is placed last to contrast with deceit (v. 22), and the best rendering is that of the NIV: "true righteousness and holiness." God could create no less (see Luke 1:75).

"Righteousness" relates to our fellow men and reflects the second table of the law (Ex. 20:12–17). "Holiness" (hosiotēs, sacred observance of all duties to God) relates to God and reflects the first table (Ex. 20:3–11). The believer, then, possesses a new nature, a new self, a holy and righteous inner person fit for the presence of God. This is the believer's truest self.

So this new self is righteous and holy, a new creation in God's image from which Paul refuses to admit any sin results. Thus his language in Romans 6–7 is explicit in placing the reality of sin other than in the new self. He says, "Do not let sin reign in your *mortal body*" (6:12) and, "Do not go on presenting the *members of your body* to sin" (6:13, emphasis added).

In those passages Paul places sin in the believer's life in the body. In Romans 7 he sees it in the flesh. He says, "No longer am I the one doing it, but sin which dwells in me" (v. 17), "Nothing good dwells in me, that is, in my flesh" (v. 18), "I am no longer the one doing it, but sin which dwells in me" (v. 20), and "the law of sin which is in my members" (v. 23).

In those texts Paul acknowledges that being a new self in the image of God does not eliminate sin. It is still present in the flesh, the body, the unredeemed humanness that includes the whole human person's thinking and behavior. But he will not allow that new inner man to be given responsibility for sin. The new "I" loves and longs for the holiness and righteousness for which it was created.

Paul summarizes the dichotomy with these words: "So then, on the one hand I myself with my mind [synonymous here with the new self] am serving the law of God, but on the other, with my flesh [synonymous here with unredeemed humanness contained in our sinful bodies] the law of sin" (Rom. 7:25). It is this struggle that prompts the anticipation for "the redemption of the body" described in Romans 8:23 (cf. Phil. 3:20–21).

We are new, but not yet *all new*. We are righteous and holy, but not yet *perfectly* righteous and holy. But understanding the genuine reality of our transforming salvation is essential if we are to know how to live as Christians in the Body of Christ to which we belong.

The remaining portions of the epistle contain exhortations to the believer to bring his body into obedience to the will of God.

Many rescue missions have a delousing room, where the homeless who have not had a bath in months discard all their old clothes and are thoroughly bathed and disinfected. The unsalvageable old clothes are burned and new clothes are issued. The now-clean clean man is provided clean clothes.

That is a picture of salvation, except that in salvation the new believer is not simply given a bath but a completely new nature. The continuing need of the Christian life is to keep discarding and burning the remnants of the old sinful clothing. "Do not go on presenting the members of your body to sin as instruments of unrighteousness," Paul pleads; "but present yourselves to God as those alive from the dead, and your members as instruments of righteousness to God" (Rom. 6:13).

The many "therefores" and "wherefores" present in the New Testament usually introduce appeals for believers to live like the new creatures they are in Christ. Because of our new life, our new Lord, our new nature, and our new power, we are *therefore* called to live a correspondingly new lifestyle.

Chapter 3

WALKING IN NEWNESS OF LIFE

ROMANS 6:1–10

What shall we say then? Are we to continue in sin that grace may increase? May it never be! How shall we who died to sin still live in it? Or do you not know that all of us who have been baptized into Christ Jesus have been baptized into His death? Therefore we have been buried with Him through baptism into death, so that as Christ was raised from the dead through the glory of the Father, so we too might walk in newness of life. For if we have become united with Him in the likeness of His death, certainly we shall also be in the likeness of His resurrection, knowing this, that our old self was crucified with Him, in order that our body of sin might be done away with, so that we would no longer be slaves to sin; for he who has died is freed from sin. Now if we have died with Christ, we believe that we shall also live with Him, knowing that Christ, having been raised from the dead, is never to die again; death no longer is master over Him. For the death that He died, He died to sin once for all; but the life that He lives, He lives to God. (Rom. 6:1–10)

In his early teens, John Newton ran away from England and joined the crew of a slave ship. Some years later he himself was given as a slave to the wife of a slave trader in Africa. He was cruelly mistreated and lived on leftovers from the woman's meals and on wild yams he dug from the ground at night. After escaping, he lived with a group of natives for a while and eventually managed to become a sea captain himself, living the most ungodly and profligate life imaginable.

But after his dramatic conversion in 1748, he returned to England and became a selfless and tireless minister of the gospel in London. He left for posterity many hymns that are still among the most popular in the world. By far the best-known and best-loved of those is *Amazing Grace*. He became the pastor of a church in England, and to this day the churchyard carries an epitaph that Newton himself wrote:

> John Newton, Clerk,
> once an infidel and libertine,
> A servant of slaves in Africa,
> was, by the rich mercy of our Lord and Savior,
> Jesus Christ,
> Preserved, restored, pardoned,
> And appointed to preach the faith
> He had long labored to destroy.[1]

How could such a debauched, self-proclaimed enemy of the faith eventually be able to say with Paul, "I thank Christ Jesus our Lord, who has strengthened me, because He considered me faithful, putting me into service, even though I was formerly a blasphemer and a persecutor and a violent aggressor. Yet I was shown mercy" (1 Tim. 1:12–13)? How could that apostle have addressed the Corinthian believers as "those who have been sanctified in Christ Jesus, saints by calling" (1 Cor. 1:2) and yet say to them, "Do you not know that the unrighteous will not inherit the kingdom of God? Do not be deceived; neither fornicators, nor idolaters, nor adulterers, nor effeminate, nor homosexuals, nor thieves, nor the covetous, nor drunkards, nor revilers, nor swindlers, will inherit the kingdom of God. *Such were some of you*" (6:9–11a; emphasis added).

Paul immediately gives the answer, reminding them that they "were justified in the name of the Lord Jesus Christ and in the Spirit of our God" (v. 11b).

It is those and similar vital concerns that Paul addresses in Romans 6–8. The apostle has finished an extensive discussion of man's sin and redemption through Christ; he now moves to the subject of the believer's holiness—the life of righteousness that God provides for His children, a life of obedience to His Word accomplished only in the power of His Spirit.

In his letter to the Galatian churches Paul gives a brief and beautiful summary of the divine principle that makes transformed life and transformed living possible: "I have been crucified with Christ; and it is no longer I who live, but Christ lives in me; and the life which I now live in the flesh I live by faith in the Son of God, who loved me and gave Himself up for me" (Gal. 2:20).

The believer is to walk in a new, transformed life, or "in newness of life" (Rom. 6:4). Paul presents three elements in his opening defense of how the believer can have a holy life, all found in the first ten verses of Romans 6: the antagonist (v. 1), the answer (v. 2), and the argument explaining and defending that answer (vv. 3–10).

THE ANTAGONISTS

What shall we say then? Are we to continue in sin that grace may increase? (6:1)

Paul anticipates the major objections of his critics. Well before the time he wrote this epistle, he and Barnabas in particular—but doubtless the other apostles, teachers, and prophets as well—had already encountered considerable opposition against the preaching of salvation by grace through faith alone. The typical religious Jew of that day could not comprehend pleasing God apart from strict adherence to the Mosaic and rabbinic law. To them, conformity to such law was the embodiment of godliness.

Some Call for Circumcision and Law-Keeping

While Paul and Barnabas were preaching in Antioch of Syria, some Jewish men who professed faith in Christ "came down from Judea and began teaching the brethren, 'Unless you are circumcised according to the custom of Moses, you cannot be saved.' And when Paul and Barnabas had great dissension and debate with them, the brethren determined that Paul and Barnabas and some others of them should go up to Jerusalem to the apostles and elders concerning this issue" (Acts 15:1–2). When the two men arrived in Jerusalem, some other Jews who claimed to be Christians, a group of legalistic Pharisees, also opposed their teaching, "saying, 'It is necessary to circumcise them [Gentile converts] and to direct them to observe the Law of Moses'" (Acts 15:5).

During the ensuing council of Jerusalem, Peter boldly declared that God "made no distinction between us [Jews] and them [Gentiles], cleansing their hearts by faith. Now therefore why do you put God to the test by placing upon the neck of the disciples a yoke which neither our fathers nor we have been able to bear? But we believe that we are saved through the grace of the Lord Jesus, in the same way as they also are" (Acts 15:9-11). After further comments by Paul and Barnabas and a summary by James, the council unanimously agreed that obedience to the Mosaic law contributed nothing to salvation and should not be made binding on any believer, Gentile or even Jew (see vv. 12-29).

Some years later, after returning to Jerusalem from collecting offerings from largely Gentile churches on behalf of needy believers in Judea, Paul sought to conciliate immature Jewish believers—as well as defuse some of the opposition from unbelieving Jews—by going to the temple to make a vow. When some unbelieving Jews from Asia saw him in the temple, they falsely assumed he had defiled the temple by bringing Gentiles into the restricted area. They nearly caused a riot in the city when they cried out, "Men of Israel, come to our aid! This is the man who preaches to all men everywhere against our people and the Law and this place; and besides he has even brought Greeks into the temple and has defiled this holy place" (Acts 21:28).

Others Celebrate Their Sin in the Name of Grace

Paul also knew that, at the opposite extreme, some readers would misinterpret his assertion that "where sin increased, grace abounded all the more" (Rom. 5:20). They would foolishly accuse him of teaching that sin itself glorifies God by causing His grace to increase. If that were true, they reasoned, then men not only are free to sin but are *obligated* to sin in order to enable God to expand His grace. If salvation is all of God and all of grace, and if God is glorified in the dispensing of grace, the sinful heart may be inclined to reason: "The more sin, the more grace; therefore, men should sin with abandon and give God more opportunity to demonstrate His grace."

That is exactly the perverted interpretation taught by the infamous Rasputin, religious adviser to the ruling Romanov family of Russia in the late nineteenth and early twentieth centuries. He taught and exemplified the antinomian view of salvation through repeated experiences of sin and false repentance. He believed that the more you sin, the more God gives you grace. So the more you sin with abandon, the more you give God the opportunity to glorify Himself. Rasputin declared that if you are simply an ordinary sinner, you are not giving God an opportunity to show His glory, so you need to be an *extraordinary* sinner.

Paul had already countered a similar hypothetical charge: "If our unrighteousness demonstrates the righteousness of God, what shall we say? The God who inflicts wrath is not unrighteous, is He? (I am speaking in human terms.)" The apostle answers his own question with an emphatic, "May it never be! For otherwise, how will God judge the world?" (Rom. 3:5–6). He then proceeds to roundly condemn those who would teach the depraved idea of "Let us do evil that good may come" (v. 8).

Legalistic Jews would charge the apostle with just that sort of *antinomianism*—of contradicting the laws of God and advocating moral and spiritual license to do as one pleases—presumably justified on the grounds that such living actually glorifies God. Those opponents had an especially hard time accepting the idea of salvation on the basis of faith alone, apart from any works. To add to that doctrine the idea that increased sin somehow increases God's grace would be to compound the anathema.

In trying to protect the faith from that danger, however, they injected another danger: the idea that salvation as well as spirituality

—even for believers in Christ—is produced by conformity to external law.

Avoiding the Extremes of Legalism and Libertinism

Throughout church history, some Christian groups have fallen into the same kind of error, insisting that conformity to countless man-made regulations and ceremony is necessary for true godliness. Whether in the form of extreme ritualism or of strictly prescribed codes of conduct, men have presumed to protect and bolster the pure gospel of grace working through faith alone by adding legalistic requirements of their own making.

The church also has always been in danger of contamination by false believers who use the freedom of the gospel as a justification for sin. As Jude declared, "For certain persons have crept in unnoticed, those who were long beforehand marked out for this condemnation, ungodly persons who turn the grace of our God into licentiousness and deny our only Master and Lord, Jesus Christ" (Jude 4).

Here Paul deals a death blow to that kind of antinomianism, yet he does so without yielding an inch of ground to those who would deny that God's grace is sufficient for salvation. Under the leadership of the Holy Spirit, the apostle avoided the extreme of legalism on the one hand and of libertinism on the other. He would neither abandon God's grace to accommodate the legalists nor abandon God's righteousness to accommodate the libertines.

As Scripture makes plain from Genesis through Revelation, a saving relationship with God is inextricably linked to holy living, and a holy life is lived by the power of God working in and through the heart of the true believer. In God's redemptive act in a person's heart, true holiness is as much a gift of God as is the new birth and the spiritual life it brings. The life that is not basically marked by holiness has no claim to salvation. It is true that no believer will be sinless until he goes to be with the Lord by death or by rapture, but a professed believer who persistently disregards Christ's lordship and His standards of righteousness by disobedience has no claim on Christ's saviorhood. It is that cardinal gospel truth that Paul forcefully defends in Romans 6–7.

In light of the pervasive antinomianism of our own day, there is no more important truth for believers to understand than the inseparable connection between justification and sanctification as salvation components. Only by having a new life in Christ can one live out the holiness Christ demands. Yet due to unbiblical teachings of easy believism (see p. 169) and the worldly lifestyles of both leaders and members, many churches who go under the banner of evangelicalism give little evidence either of redemption or of the holiness that necessarily accompanies saving grace.

"What shall we say then to such foolish assertions?" the apostle asks, adding rhetorically, "Are we to continue in sin that grace might increase?" *Epimenō* ("to continue") carries the idea of habitual persistence. It was sometimes used of a person's purposely living in a certain place and of making it his permanent residence. It is the word that John used of the determined Jewish leaders who persisted in trying to induce Jesus to contradict the law of Moses (John 8:7).

Paul was not speaking of a believer's occasional falling into sin, as every Christian does at times because of the weakness and imperfection of the flesh. He was speaking of intentional, willful sinning as an established pattern of life.

Before salvation, sin *cannot* be anything but the established way of life, because sin at best taints everything the unredeemed person does. But the believer, who has a new life and is indwelt by God's own Spirit, has no excuse to continue habitually in sin. Can he then possibly live in the same submissive relationship to sin that he had before salvation? Put in theological terms, can justification truly exist apart from sanctification? Can a person receive a new life and continue in his old way of living? Does the divine transaction of redemption have no continuing and sustaining power in those who are redeemed? Put still another way, can a person who persists in living as a child of Satan have been truly born again as a child of God? Many say yes. Paul says no, as verse 2 emphatically states.

THE ANSWER

May it never be! How shall we who died to sin still live in it? (6:2)

Immediately answering his own question, Paul exclaims with obvious horror, "May it never be!" *Mē genoito* is literally and accurately translated "May it never be," and it was the strongest idiom of repudiation in New Testament Greek. It is used fourteen times in Paul's letters alone. The apostle has already used it three times in chapter 3 of Romans (vv. 4, 6, 31) and will use it another six times before he concludes (see 6:15; 7:7, 13; 9:14; 11:1, 11). It carries the sense of outrage that an idea of this kind could ever be thought of as true.

The very suggestion that sin could in any conceivable way please and glorify God was abhorrent to Paul. The falsehood is almost too self-evident to be given the dignity of detailed refutation. Instead it deserves only condemnation.

An Arresting Rhetorical Question

But lest his readers think he might be evading a difficult problem, the apostle seems almost to shout why the notion that sin brings glory to God is repugnant and preposterous. At this point he does not respond with reasoned argument but with a brief and arresting rhetorical question: "How shall we who died to sin still live in it?"

Paul does not recognize his antagonists' assertion as having the least credence or merit. He does not now argue the truth but merely declares it. The person who is alive in Christ has "died to sin," and it is inconceivable and self-contradictory to propose that a believer can henceforth live in the sin from which he was delivered by death. God's grace is given for the very purpose of saving from sin, and only the most corrupt mind using the most perverted logic could argue that continuing in the sin from which he has supposedly been saved somehow honors the holy God who sacrificed His only Son to deliver men and women from all unrighteousness.

By simple reason it must be admitted that the person who has died to one kind of life cannot still live in it. The apostle Paul was not speaking of the present state of the believer as daily dying to sin but the past act (*apothnēskō*, second aorist active) of being dead to sin. Paul is saying it is impossible for a Christian to remain in a *constant* state of sinfulness. The act is in this sense once and for all.

Again by definition, a person does not continually die. If his death is real, it is permanent. The person who has truly died to sin cannot possibly still live in it. Both in the spiritual as well as the physical realms, death and life are incompatible. Both logically and theologically, therefore, spiritual life cannot coexist with spiritual death. The idea that Christians can continue to live habitually in sin not only is unbiblical but irrational. They may lapse into sinful behavior at times, which grieves the Holy Spirit, but they will not practice sin regularly. Christians obviously are able to commit many of the sins they committed before salvation, but they are *not* able to live perpetually in those sins as they did before. "No one who is born of God practices sin," John declares, "because His seed abides in him; and he cannot sin, because he is born of God" (1 John 3:9). It is not merely that Christians *should not* continue to live in the realm and dimension of sin but that they *cannot*.

The apostle does not equivocate about the superabundance of God's grace. But the truth that "where sin increased, grace abounded all the more" (5:20b) obviously focuses on and magnifies God's grace, not man's sin. It declares that no single sin is too great for God to forgive and that even the collective sins of all mankind for all ages—past, present, and future—are more than sufficiently covered by the measureless abundance of God's grace activated in the atonement.

The Unbroken Continuum: God's Divine Work of Redemption

Paul goes on to declare without equivocation that a genuinely justified life both is and will *continue to be* a sanctified life. For the purposes of systematic theology and to make God's work of redemption somewhat more comprehensible to finite human minds, we often speak of sanctification as following justification. There is, of course, a sense in which it does, in that justification involves what is often called a forensic, or legal, declaration of righteousness that is immediate, complete, and eternal. But justification and sanctification are not separate stages in salvation; rather, they are different aspects of the unbroken continuum of God's divine work of redemption in a believer's life by which He not only declares a person righteous but recreates him to become righteous. Holiness is as much a work of God in the believer as any other element of redemption. When a person is redeemed, God not only declares him righteous, but also begins to develop Christ's righteousness in him. Thus salvation is not merely a legal transaction, but results inevitably in a miracle of transformation.

Growing in the Christian life is always a process, not to be perfected "until the day of Christ Jesus" (Phil. 1:6). But there is no such thing as a true convert to Christ in whom justification has been accomplished but in whom sanctification, both forensic and practical, has not already begun. In other words, there is *never* a division between justification and sanctification. There is, however, always and inevitably a total and permanent division between the old self and the new self. In Christ, the old self has been made a corpse; and a corpse, by definition, has in it no remaining vestige of life.

The old man, the old self, is the unregenerate person. He is not part righteous and part sinful, but totally sinful and without the slightest potential *within himself* for becoming righteous and pleasing to God. The new man, on the other hand, is the regenerate person. He is made pleasing to God through Jesus Christ and his new nature is *entirely godly and righteous*. He is not yet perfected or glorified, but he is already spiritually alive and holiness is at work in him. The new man *will continue* to grow in that holiness, no matter how slowly or falteringly, because, by its very nature, life grows. Barnhouse wrote, "Holiness starts where justification finishes, and if holiness does not start, we have the right to suspect that justification never started either."[2]

There is therefore simply no such thing as justification without sanctification. There is no such thing as divine life without divine living. The truly saved person lives a new and godly life in a new and godly realm. He now and forever lives in God's realm of grace and righteousness and can never again live in Satan's realm of self and sin. As the natural, sinful, unregenerate man cannot restrain the manifestation of what he is, neither can the regenerate man.

Again, salvation not only is a transaction but a transformation, not only forensic but actual. Christ died not only for what we did but for what we are. Paul tells believers: "For you have died and your life is hidden with Christ in God" (Col. 3:3). Even more explicitly he declares that "if anyone is in Christ, he is a new creature; the old things passed away; behold, new things have come" (2 Cor. 5:17).

And so the phrase "died to sin" expresses the fundamental premise of this entire chapter in Romans, the rest of which is essentially an elaboration of that cardinal reality. It is impossible to be alive in Christ and also still be alive to sin. It is not that a believer at any moment before going to be with Christ is totally without sin, but that from the moment he is born again he is totally separated from the controlling power of sin, the sin life from which Christ died to deliver him. The sense in which this crucial fact is true unfolds in the following text.

THE ARGUMENT

Or do you not know that all of us who have been baptized into Christ Jesus have been baptized into His death? Therefore we have been buried with Him through baptism into death, in order that as Christ was raised from the dead through the glory of the Father, so we too might walk in newness of life. For if we have become united with Him in the likeness of His death, certainly we shall be also in the likeness of His resurrection, knowing this, that our old self was crucified with Him, in order that our body of sin might be done away with, so that we would no longer be slaves to sin; for he who has died is freed from sin.

Now if we have died with Christ, we believe that we shall also live with Him, knowing that Christ, having been raised

from the dead, is never to die again; death no longer is master over Him. For the death that He died, He died to sin once for all; but the life that He lives, He lives to God. (Rom. 6:3–10)

The idea that a believer can glorify God by continuing in sin apparently was pervasive in the Roman churches and elsewhere, or Paul would not have given it such attention. In a series of four logical and sequential principles, he reasons from his basic point made in verse 2 that the person who has died to sin cannot continue to live in it.

We are Baptized into Christ
Or do you not know that all of us . . . have been baptized into Christ Jesus (6:3a)

The first principle is that all true Christians have been baptized into Christ Jesus.

When John the Baptist baptized in water for repentance of sin, the clear and obvious intent was a turning to righteousness. In receiving John's baptism, the sinner renounced his sin and through symbolic cleansing henceforth identified himself with the Messiah and His righteousness. Baptism uniquely represented identification.

Wuest defines this particular use of *baptizō* (to be baptized) as "the introduction or placing of a person or thing into a new environment or into union with something else so as to alter its condition or its relationship to its previous environment or condition."[3]

In his first letter to the Corinthian church, Paul spoke of Israel's being baptized into Moses (1 Cor. 10:2), symbolizing the people's identity or solidarity with Moses as God's spokesman and leader and the placing of themselves under his authority. By that identity and submission they participated in the leadership and consequent blessings and honor of Moses. The faithful Israelite was, as it were, fused with Moses, who was fused with God. In a similar but infinitely more profound and permanent way, "all of us," that is, all Christians, "have been baptized into Christ Jesus," thus permanently being immersed into Him, so as to be made one with Him. It should be noted here that the Greek term as well as the concept call for water baptism being by immersion in order to symbolize this reality properly.

In other passages, Paul affirmed the importance of water baptism in obedience to the Lord's direct command (see 1 Cor. 1:13–17 and Eph. 4:5). But that is only the outward symbol of the baptism to which the apostle refers here. He is speaking metaphorically of the spiritual immersion of believers into Christ through the Holy Spirit, of the believer's intimate oneness with his divine Lord. It is the truth of which Jesus spoke when He said, "Lo, I am with you always, even to the end of the age" (Matt. 28:20), and which John describes as "our fellowship . . . with the Father, and with His Son Jesus Christ" (1 John 1:3). To the Corinthians, Paul speaks of it as the believer's being one spirit with Christ (1 Cor. 6:17), and to the Galatian believers he explains that "all of you who were baptized into Christ have clothed yourselves with Christ" (Gal. 3:27). In each instance, the idea is that of being totally encompassed by and unified with Christ.

It is in light of that incomprehensible truth that Paul so strongly rebukes the sexual immorality of some of the Corinthian believers, exclaiming incredulously, "Do you not know that your bodies are members of Christ? Shall I then take away the members of Christ and make them members of a prostitute? May it never be!" (1 Cor. 6:15).

As noted above, salvation not only is God's reckoning a sinner as righteous but of *granting* him a new, righteous disposition or nature. The believer's righteousness in Christ is an earthly as well as a heavenly reality, or else it is not a reality at all. His new life is a divine life. That is why it is impossible for a true believer to continue to live in the same sinful way in which he lived before being saved.

Many people interpret Paul's argument in Romans 6:3–10 as referring to water baptism. However, Paul is simply using the physical analogy of water baptism to teach the spiritual reality of the believer's union with Christ. Water baptism is the outward identification of an inward reality—faith in Jesus' death, burial, and resurrection. Paul was not advocating salvation by water baptism; that would have contradicted everything he had just said about salvation by grace and not works in Romans 3–5, which has no mention of water baptism.

Water baptism was a public symbol of faith in God. The apostle Peter said baptism is a mark of salvation because it gives outward evidence of an inward faith in Christ (1 Peter 3:21). Titus says the same thing in Titus 3:4–5: "But when the kindness of God our Savior and His love for mankind appeared, He saved us, not on the basis of deeds which we have done in righteousness, but according to His mercy, by the washing of regeneration and renewing by the Holy Spirit." Paul says in Acts 22:16, "Now why do you delay? Get up and be baptized, and wash away your sins, calling on His name." Those verses are not saying a person is saved by water but that water baptism is a symbol of genuine saving faith.

The Roman believers were well aware of the symbol of baptism. When Paul says "Do you not know . . . ?" he is in effect saying, "Are you ignorant of the meaning of your own baptism? Have you forgotten what your baptism symbolized?" They were unaware that water baptism symbolizes the spiritual reality of being immersed into Jesus Christ. The tragedy is that many mistake the symbol of water baptism as the means of salvation rather than the demonstration of it. To turn a symbol into the reality is to eliminate the reality, which in this case is salvation by grace through faith in Christ alone.

We Are Identified in Christ's Death and Resurrection

. . . have been baptized into His death? Therefore we have been buried with Him through baptism into death, so that as Christ was raised from the dead through the glory of the Father, so we too might walk in newness of life. For if we have become united with Him in the likeness of His death, certainly we shall also be in the likeness of His resurrection, (6:3b–5)

The second principle Paul emphasizes is an extension of the first. All Christians not only are identified with Christ but are identified with Him specifically in His death and resurrection.

The initial element of the second principle is that all true believers "have been baptized into His [Christ's] death." That is a historical fact looking back to our union with Him on the cross. And the reason "we have been buried with Him through baptism into death [is] that as Christ was raised from the dead through the glory of the Father, so we too might walk in newness of life." That is a historical fact looking back to our union with Him in resurrection.

That truth is far too wondrous for us to understand fully, but the basic and obvious reality of it is that we died with Christ in order that we might have life through Him and live like Him. Again Paul emphasizes not so much the immorality but the impossibility of our continuing to live the way we did before we were saved. By trusting in Jesus Christ as Lord and Savior, we were, by an unfathomable divine miracle, taken back two thousand years, as it were, and made to participate in our Savior's death and to be buried with Him, burial being the proof of death. The purpose of that divine act of bringing us through death (which paid the penalty for our sin) and resurrection with Christ was to enable us henceforth to walk in newness of life.

The noble theologian Charles Hodge summarized, "There can be no participation in Christ's life without a participation in His death, and we cannot enjoy the benefits of His death unless we are partakers of the power of His life. We must be reconciled to God in order to be holy, and we cannot be reconciled without thereby becoming holy."[4]

As Christ's resurrection life was the certain consequence of His death as the sacrifice for our sin, so the believer's holy life in Christ is the certain consequence of his death to sin in Christ.

"Newness" is translated from *kairos*, which refers to newness of quality and character, not *neos*, which refers merely to newness in point of time. Just as sin characterized our old life, so righteousness now characterizes our new life. Scripture is filled with descriptions of the believer's new spiritual life. We are said to receive a new heart (Ezek. 36:26), a new spirit (Ezek. 18:31), a new song (Ps. 40:3), and a new name (Rev. 2:17). We are called a new creation (2 Cor. 5:17), a new creature (Gal. 6:15), and a new self (Eph. 4:24).

Continuing to affirm the truth that this union with Christ in His death brings new life and also inevitably brings a new way of living, Paul says, "For if we have become united with Him in the likeness of His death, certainly we shall also be in the likeness of His resurrection." In other words, as an old life died, so a new one was necessarily born.

Handley Moule graphically asserted,

We have "received the reconciliation" that we may now walk, not away from God, as if released from a prison, but with God, as His children in His Son. Because we are justified, we are to be holy, separated from sin, separated to God; not as a mere indication that our faith is real, and that therefore we are legally safe, but because we were justified for this very purpose, that we might be holy. . . .

The grapes upon a vine are not merely a living token that the tree is a vine and is alive; they are the product for which the vine exists. It is a thing not to be thought of that the sinner should accept justification and live to himself. It is a moral contradiction of the very deepest kind, and cannot be entertained without betraying an initial error in the man's whole spiritual creed.[5]

Our Body of Sin Has Been Destroyed

knowing this, that our old self was crucified with Him, in order that our body of sin might be done away with, so that we would no longer be slaves to sin; for he who has died is freed from sin. (6:6–7)

The third principle Paul stresses is that the old sinful self has been killed. The phrase "knowing this" obviously is an appeal to what should be common knowledge among believers, those to and of whom Paul is speaking. "You should be well aware," he was saying, "that in Christ you are not the same people you were before salvation. You have new life, a new heart, a new spiritual strength, a new hope, and countless other new things that had no part in your former life." When Christ redeemed us, "our old self was crucified," that is, put to death and destroyed.

In this case, 'old' is not from the Greek *archaios*, which simply refers to chronological age, but rather *palaios*, which refers to something that is completely worn out and useless, fit only for the scrap heap. For all practical purposes it is destroyed. In a passage quoted above from Colossians, Paul declares "I have been crucified with Christ"—that is, my old "I" is dead and no longer exists—"and it is no longer I who live, but Christ lives in me" (Gal. 2:20). In other words, our new life as Christians is not a made-over old life but a new divinely-bestowed life that is Christ's very own.

When Scripture is compared with Scripture, as a responsible study of Scripture always includes, it becomes clear that the "old self" to which Paul refers in Romans 6 is none other than the unregenerate, in-Adam man described in Romans 5, the person who is apart from divine redemption and the new life it brings.

The dualistic view that a Christian has two natures uses unbiblical terminology and can lead to a perception that is extremely destructive to holy living. Some who hold such views go to the extreme of the Gnostics in Paul's day, claiming that because the evil self cannot be controlled or changed and because it is going to be destroyed in the future anyway, it does not much matter what you let it do. It is only "spiritual" things, such as your thoughts and intentions, that are of significance. It is not surprising that in congregations where such a philosophy reigns, immoral conduct among the membership as well as the leadership is common and church discipline is usually nonexistent.

Paul asserts that such a perverted view of Christian liberty is known by well-taught believers to be false and destructive and that it should be condemned out-of-hand in the church. In Romans 6:6, Paul mentions three marvelous truths that should protect believers from such false views about the old and new natures.

The first truth is that "our old self was crucified with Him," that is, with Christ. Crucifixion does not simply produce extreme suffering; it produces death. To be crucified is to die. The old self of every believer was crucified with his Lord, or else he has not been saved. There is no such thing as a true Christian who has not died with Christ.

In Ephesians, Paul writes in some detail about the "old self" or the old man. He tells believers: "But you did not learn Christ in this way, if indeed you have heard Him and have been taught in Him, just as truth is in Jesus, that, in reference to your former manner of life, you lay aside the old self, which is being corrupted in accordance with the lusts of deceit, and that you be renewed in the spirit of your mind, and put on the new self, which in the likeness of God has been created in righteousness and holiness of the truth" (Eph. 4:20–24). The Christian's *new self* is actually in God's own likeness!

As John Murray and other New Testament scholars have pointed out, both "lay aside" (v. 22) and "put on" (v. 24) translate Greek infinitives that in this context should be rendered as infinitives of result. In other words, Paul is not giving an admonition or command but rather a statement of fact about what has already been accomplished. Murray therefore translates verse 22 as, "So that ye have put off according to the former manner life the old man."[6]

Moule translated that verse as, "Our old man, our old state, as out of Christ and under Adam's headship, under guilt and in moral bondage, was crucified with Christ."[7] Still another expositor and commentator, Martyn Lloyd-Jones, rendered the verse: "Do not go on living as if you were still that old man, because that old man has died. Do not go on living as if he was still there."[8]

Even if verse 22 is taken as a command, it would not be a command to reject the dictates of our old self—which the apostle has just declared has been crucified and is now dead, and therefore cannot dictate to us anymore. It would rather be a command for us not to follow the remaining memories of its sinful ways, as if we were still under its evil mastery.

Declaring again that true believers have already been removed from the presence and control of the old sinful self, Paul tells the Galatian church, "Those who belong to Christ Jesus *have crucified* the flesh with its passions and desires" (Gal. 5:24; emphasis added).

In a somewhat parallel passage in Colossians, Paul clearly states that a believer's putting off the old self is a *fait accompli*, something that has already and irreversibly been accomplished. "Do not lie to one another," he says, "since you laid aside the old self with its evil practices, and have put on the new self who is being renewed to a true knowledge according to the image of the One who created him" (Col. 3:9–10). It was not that every Colossian believer was fully mature and had managed to gain complete mastery over the residual old self. Paul was saying rather that *every* believer, at any level of maturity, can claim that his old self *already has been* laid aside "with its evil practices." In exactly the same way, his new self in Christ is already "being renewed" into conformity with the very image of the God who has recreated him.

The second great truth Paul gives in Romans 6:6 about the old and new dispositions is that "our body of sin might be done away with." The phrase *might be* does not here carry the idea of possibility but is simply an idiomatic way of stating an already existing fact. In other words, our historical death to sin at the cross in Christ results in our sin being done away with. Those truths are so nearly synonymous that verse 6 is almost a tautology, true by virtue of logic alone. Sin that is dead (crucified) is obviously done away with. Paul states the truth in those two different ways in order to make his point more understandable and to remove any possible ambiguity.

Both the NASB ("done away with") and the KJV ("destroyed") can suggest that our body of sin is annihilated. But the Greek word *katargeō* that is translated "done away with" literally means "to render inoperative or invalid," to make something ineffective by removing its power of control. That meaning is seen clearly in the term's rendering in such other passages in Romans as 3:3, 31 ("nullify"), 4:14 ("nullified"), 7:2 ("released from").

As every mature Christian learns, the more one grows in Christ, the more he becomes aware of sin in his life. In many places, Paul uses the terms *body* and *flesh* to refer to sinful propensities that are intertwined with physical weaknesses and pleasures (e.g., Rom. 8:10-11, 13, 23). New birth in Christ brings death to the sinful self, but it does not bring death to the temporal flesh and its corrupted inclinations until the future glorification. Obviously, a Christian's body is potentially good and is intended to do only good things, else Paul would not have commanded believers to present their bodies to God as "a living and holy sacrifice, acceptable to God" (Rom. 12:1). It can respond to the new holy disposition, but does not always do so.

As Paul explains more fully in Romans 7, a believer's unredeemed humanness—of which he uses his own as example—remains with him until he is transformed to heavenly glory. And, as both Scripture and experience clearly teach, the remaining humanness somehow retains certain weaknesses and propensities to sin. The tyranny and penalty of sin both in and over the Christian's life have been broken, but sin's potential for expression in his life has not yet been fully removed. His human weaknesses and instincts make him capable of succumbing to Satan's temptations when he lives apart from the Spirit's Word and power. He is a new, redeemed, holy creation incarcerated in unredeemed flesh.

To combat that remaining weakness in regard to sin, the apostle admonishes believers later in the present chapter: "Just as you presented your members as slaves to impurity and to lawlessness, resulting in further lawlessness, so now present your members as slaves to righteousness, resulting in sanctification" (Rom. 6:19).

The third great truth Paul gives in verse 6 about the old and new natures is that "we should no longer be slaves to sin." Again, the translation leaves the meaning somewhat ambiguous. But as the apostle makes unequivocal a few verses later, "Thanks be to God that though you were slaves of sin, you *became obedient* from the heart to that form of teaching to which you were committed, and *having been freed from sin*, you *became slaves of righteousness*" (Rom. 6:17–18; emphasis added). All the verbs in those two verses make clear that a believer's slavery under sin has already been broken by Christ and is henceforth a thing of the past. Several verses later, Paul reiterates the truth that the believer's new enslavement to righteousness is made possible because he *is now* enslaved to God (v. 22; emphasis added).

In other words, the immediate context of "should no longer be slaves of sin" carries the more precise—and extremely significant—meaning that believers *can* "no longer be slaves of sin." As already noted, Paul does not teach that a Christian is no longer *capable* of committing sin but that he no longer is under the compulsion and tyranny of sin, nor will he dutifully and solely obey sin as he formerly did. For all genuine Christians, *slavery* to sin no longer exists.

The reason, of course, is that "he who has died is freed from sin." Because the old life "has died," what characterized the old life has died with it, most importantly slavery to sin, from which *all* the redeemed in Christ are once and forever freed.

In his first epistle, Peter strongly emphasizes that truth. "Therefore, since Christ has suffered in the flesh," he says, "arm yourselves also with the same purpose, because he who has suffered in the flesh has ceased from sin, so as to live the rest of the time in the flesh no longer for the lusts of men, but for the will of God" (1 Pet. 4:1–2). Peter is not, however, teaching sinless perfection in this present earthly life, because he goes on to give the severe warning: "By no means let any of you suffer as a murderer, or thief, or evildoer, or a troublesome meddler" (v. 15).

Lloyd-Jones offers a helpful illustration of the believer's relation to his old sinful disposition.[9] He pictures two adjoining fields, one owned by Satan and one owned by God, that are separated by a road. Before salvation, a person lives in Satan's field and is totally subject to his jurisdiction. After salvation, a person works in the other field, now subject only to God's jurisdiction. As he plows in the new field, however, the believer is often cajoled by his former master, who seeks to entice him back into the old sinful ways. Satan often succeeds in temporarily drawing the believer's attention away from his new Master and his new way of life. But he is powerless to draw the believer back into the old field of sin and death.

The One Death of Christ Was a Death to Sin

Now if we have died with Christ, we believe that we shall also live with Him, knowing that Christ, having been raised from the dead, is never to die again; death no longer is master over Him. For the death that He died, He died to sin once for all; but the life that He lives, He lives to God. (Rom. 6:8–10)

The fourth principle is that Christ's one death to sin brought not only the death of sin but the death of death itself for those who, by faith, have died with Him. These three verses are essentially a summary of what Paul has just been teaching about the believer's death to sin and his new life in Christ. He also stresses the permanence of that awesome and glorious truth.

The assurance that "we shall also live with Him" obviously applies to the believer's ultimate and eternal presence with Christ in heaven. But the context, which focuses on holy living, strongly suggests that Paul is here speaking primarily about our living with Him in righteousness in this present life. In Greek, as in English, future tenses often carry the idea of certainty. That seems to be the case with Paul's use of *suzaō* (or *sunzaō*), here rendered "shall also live." As the apostle makes clear in verse 10 in regard to Christ, he is not merely speaking of existing in the presence of God but of living to God, that is, living a life fully consistent with God's holiness.

Building on that thought, Paul goes on to say, "knowing that Christ, having been raised from the dead, is never to die again; death no longer is master over Him." The point is that, because *we* have died and been raised with Christ (vv. 3–5), we, too, shall "never die again." The sin that made us subject to death is no longer master over us, just as it "no longer is master over Him." It also can never be our executioner.

The climax of this section of chapter 6 is that "the death that [Christ] died, He died to sin, once for all; but the life that He lives, He lives to God." Because death is the penalty of sin (Rom. 6:23), to break the mastery of sin is to break the mastery of death.

Two extremely important truths in verse 10 should be emphasized. The first is that Christ "died to sin." Having lived a perfectly sinless life during His incarnation, Christ obviously never had the same relationship to sin that every other human being has. He not only was never mastered by sin but never committed a sin of the least sort. How then, we wonder, could *He* have died to sin? Yet it is clear from this verse that in whatever way Christ died to sin, believers also have died to sin.

Some suggest that believers have died to sin in the sense of no longer being sensitive to the allurements of sin. But that view is not borne out by Christian experience, and it obviously could not apply to Christ, who was never, in the first place, sensitive to sin's allurements. Others suggest that Paul is teaching that believers *ought* to die to sin. But again, such an interpretation could not apply to Christ. Nor could it mean that Christ died to sin by becoming perfect, because He was always perfect.

It seems that Paul means two things in declaring that Christ "died to sin." First, He died to the *penalty* of sin by taking upon Himself the sins of the whole world. He met sin's legal demand for all mankind who would trust in Him. By their faith in Him, empowered by His divine and limitless grace, believers have forensically died to sin. Second, Christ died to the *power* of sin, forever breaking its power over those who belong to God through their faith in His Son. Paul assured even the immature and sin-prone believers in Corinth that God "made Him who knew no sin to be sin on our behalf, so that we might become the righteousness of God in Him" (2 Cor. 5:21).

It was perhaps the twin truth that believers die both to the penalty as well as to the power of sin that Augustus Toplady had in mind in the beautiful line from his great hymn *Rock of Ages*—"Be of sin the double cure, save from wrath and make me pure."

The second crucial emphasis in verse 10 is that Christ "died to sin, once for all." He achieved a victory that will never need repeating, a profound truth that the writer of Hebrews stresses again and again (7:26–27; 9:12, 28; 10:10; cf. 1 Pet. 3:18).

In addition to being actually identified with Christ in the ways

Paul mentions in this passage—namely, His death and resurrection, the destruction of the body of sin, and the death to sin—believers are also analogically likened to their Lord in His virgin birth, in that both He in His physical birth and they in their spiritual births have been conceived by the Holy Spirit. He identified with our humanity in His incarnation; then through His circumcision He placed Himself temporarily under the authority of the Mosaic law in order to redeem those under the law (Col. 2:11). We also relate to our Lord in His sufferings, as we, like Paul, bear the marks of suffering for Him.

In so many ways, believers are so completely and inextricably identified with the Lord Jesus Christ that He is not ashamed to call them brothers and sisters (Heb. 2:11 NIV).

—⊶∞⊷—

Chapter 4

WALKING BY THE SPIRIT

GALATIANS 5:16–25

But I say, walk by the Spirit, and you will not carry out the desire of the flesh. For the flesh sets its desire against the Spirit, and the Spirit against the flesh; for these are in opposition to one another, so that you may not do the things that you please. But if you are led by the Spirit, you are not under the Law. Now the deeds of the flesh are evident, which are: immorality, impurity, sensuality, idolatry, sorcery, enmities, strife, jealousy, outbursts of anger, disputes, dissensions, factions, envying, drunkenness, carousing, and things like these, of which I forewarn you, just as I have forewarned you, that those who practice such things will not inherit the kingdom of God. But the fruit of the Spirit is love, joy, peace, patience, kindness, goodness, faithfulness, gentleness, self-control; against such things there is no law. Now those who belong to Christ Jesus have crucified the flesh with its passions and desires. If we live by the Spirit, let us also walk by the Spirit. (5:16–25)

Just as Jesus Christ is the primary Person behind justification, the Holy Spirit is the primary Person behind sanctification.

A believer can no more sanctify himself than he could have saved himself in the first place. He cannot live the Christian life by his own resources any more than he could have saved himself by his own resources.

In its most profound yet simple definition, the faithful Christian life is a life directed and empowered by the Spirit. That is the theme of Galatians 5:16–25, in which Paul tells believers to "walk by the Spirit" (vv. 16, 25) and to be "led by the Spirit" (v. 18). This section might be outlined under four headings: the command, the conflict, the contrast, and the conquest.

THE COMMAND

But I say, walk by the Spirit, and you will not carry out the desire of the flesh. (5:16)

The contrasting themes of the book of Galatians are law and grace, which Paul repeatedly shows are incompatible, either as means of salvation or of sanctification. A person cannot come to God by means of law-keeping nor can he sustain living for God by keeping the law, not even the God-given law of Moses in which the Old Covenant centered.

Because no man can perfectly obey the law, it was never intended to be a means of salvation. Instead, it was given by God (1) to reveal God's holy standards and (2) to make people despair of their own failing human efforts at pleasing Him. The law's ultimate purpose was to drive men and women to Jesus Christ, who alone by grace can make them acceptable to the Father. Through the law, "the Scripture has shut up everyone under sin, so that the promise by faith in Jesus Christ might be given to those who believe" (Gal.

3:22). The law was never meant to be a savior, but only a tutor to lead men to the Savior (v. 24).

The believer has no use for the law as a means of salvation, because through Christ he has already been saved and adopted into God's heavenly household as a son (Gal. 3:26). Nor does he need the governmental system of law to guide him in his new life, because he has Christ's own Spirit as his permanent, indwelling Guide. In fact, the more a believer attempts to force himself to live by rules and regulations, no matter how lofty they may be, the more he stifles the work of the Holy Spirit.

Although Bible study, prayer, worship, witnessing, and certain behavior standards are commanded of believers and are essential to faithful Christian living, spirituality cannot be measured by how often or how intensely we are involved in such things. To use them as measures of spirituality is to become entrapped in legalism, whose only significance is in the outward, the visible, the humanly measurable. To live solely by a set of laws is to live by the flesh in self-righteousness and hypocrisy and to suppress the Spirit, who alone is able inwardly to produce works of true righteousness. Holiness comes only from the Holy Spirit. Holy living does not come from our performance for God but from *His* performance through us by His own Spirit. Holy living is "to be strengthened with power through His Spirit in the inner man" as we are "filled with the Spirit" (Eph. 3:16; 5:18).

All a Christian absolutely needs to live a holy life according to the will of God is the Holy Spirit, who is given the moment he believes (Rom. 8:9). Even the newest, most untaught Christian is indwelt by God's own resident Teacher and Strengthener. Although the Spirit uses Scripture to assist believers to grow in truth and holiness, He Himself is the supreme source of those virtues (cf. Col. 3:16).

Only pride or ignorance could lead a believer to live by an outward list of rules and commands in his own limited and sinful power when he can live by the perfect and fully sufficient inner power of the Holy Spirit. Yet that is what many believers in the Galatian churches were trying to do, and what many believers since that time have also endeavored to do.

Walking—A Way of Life

The fact that *peripateō* ("walk") is used here in the present tense indicates that Paul is speaking of continuous, regular action, in other words, a habitual way of life. And the fact that the verb is also in the imperative mood indicates he is not giving believers an option but a command.

Among other things, walking implies progress, going from where one is to where he ought to be. As a believer submits to the Spirit's control, he moves forward in his spiritual life. Step by step the Spirit moves him from where he is toward where God wants him to be. So while it is the Spirit who is the source of all holy living, it is the believer who is commanded to walk. This is the apparent paradox of the divine and human that is seen in salvation (John 6:35–40), in Scripture inspiration (cf. 1 John 1:1–3 with 2 Pet. 1:19–21), in eternal security (cf. Rom. 8:31–39 with Col. 1:21–23), and even in ministry (Col. 1:28–29).

In emphasizing the central work of the Holy Spirit in the believer's life, some Christians have lost the tension between the human and the divine and have taught the idea suggested in such popular expressions as "Let go and let God" and "the surrendered life." Rightly used, such expressions can be helpful. If they are understood to mean letting go of one's own resources and self-will and surrendering to God's truth and power, the idea is scriptural.

But if, as is often the case, they are used to teach the idea that Christian living is little more than passive submission and yieldedness to God, they are contrary to all the militant terms and commands for great effort and commitment that pervade the New Testament (see, e.g., 1 Cor. 9:24–27; Heb. 12:1–3).

If human will and actions did not play a direct and aggressive part in the Christian life, the New Testament would contain only this one instruction for believers: walk by the Spirit. Every other command would be superfluous. That is essentially the theology of what is often called quietism, of which the old Quakers were the best-known advocates. The Keswick tradition, the preaching of the famous evangelist Charles Finney, and Hannah Whitall Smith's *The Christian's Secret of a Happy Life* also reflect a strong quietistic orientation. Passive surrender to God is taught to the almost total exclusion of human volition and action.

Many advocates of a moderate quietistic approach have been godly saints and greatly used by the Lord. But the unbalanced emphasis of their teaching tends to inhibit rather than enhance the work of the Spirit. It runs the danger of underplaying, if not actually contradicting, the many other New Testament commands to believers besides that of submitting to the Holy Spirit.

The Power of the Spirit

The *power* for Christian living is entirely from the Holy Spirit, just as the power of salvation is entirely in Jesus Christ. But both in the justifying work of Christ and in the sanctifying work of the Holy Spirit, man's will is active and commitment is called for.

The Christian is not to sit on the sidelines, as it were, and simply watch the Holy Spirit do battle for him. He is called to consider himself "to be dead to sin, but alive to God in Christ Jesus," to refuse to let "sin reign in [his] mortal body," to resist presenting "the members of [his] body to sin as instruments of unrighteousness," and rather to present them "as instruments of righteousness to God" (Rom. 6:11–13). "Let us not lose heart in doing good," Paul says later in this letter, "for in due time we will reap if we do not grow weary. So then, while we have opportunity, let us do good to all people, and especially to those who are of the household of the faith" (Gal. 6:9–10).

The believer who is led by the Holy Spirit must be willing to go where the Spirit guides him and do what the Spirit leads him to do. To claim surrender to the Holy Spirit but not be personally involved in God's work is to call Jesus, "Lord, Lord," and not do what He says (Luke 6:46).

"By the Spirit, . . . you will not carry out the desire of the flesh" The Greek word used for "desire," *epithurnia,* can refer to a strong, compelling *desire* of any sort, good or evil. In this verse it is employed in relation to the evil will of the flesh bent on damnation. In verse 17 the term is used both in relation to the evil will of the flesh and in relation to the holy will of the Spirit.

To walk by the Spirit and thereby not carry out the desire of the flesh articulates the same principle as to "put on the Lord Jesus Christ, and make no provision for the flesh in regard to its lusts" (Rom. 13:14). To walk by the Spirit is to "behave properly as in the day," whereas to carry out the desire of the flesh involves such things as "carousing, . . . drunkenness, . . . sexual promiscuity and sensuality, . . . strife and jealousy" (v. 13). The two behaviors are mutually exclusive, so that at all times in our Christian lives we are either walking by the Spirit or are functioning in fleshly desire, but never both at the same time.

The life walked by the Spirit is the Christlike life, the saturation of a believer's thoughts with the truth, love, and glory of His Lord and the desire to be like Him in every way. It is to live in continual consciousness of His presence and will, letting "the word of Christ richly dwell within you" (Col. 3:16). Life walked by the Spirit is life patterned after the teaching and example of the Lord Jesus Christ. It is a life whose constant, overriding desire is to "be found in Him, ... having a righteousness ... which is through faith in Christ, the righteousness which comes from God on the basis of faith" and the desire to "know Him, and the power of His resurrection and the fellowship of His sufferings" (Phil. 3:9-10). Surely, it is no different from being "filled with the Spirit" (Eph. 5:18), a phrase referring to the controlling power exerted by the Spirit on a willing Christian.[1]

THE CONFLICT

For the flesh sets its desire against the Spirit, and the Spirit against the flesh; for these are in opposition to one another, so that you may not do the things that you please. But if you are led by the Spirit, you are not under the Law. (5:17-18)

Along with many others in the New Testament, these two verses make it obvious that walking by the Spirit is not simply a matter of passive surrender. The Spirit-led life is a life of conflict, because it is in constant combat with the old ways of the flesh that continue to tempt and seduce the believer. "The flesh sets its desire against the Spirit, and the Spirit against the flesh."

The Nature of Our Flesh

It should be noted that "the flesh" is the term Paul often uses to describe what remains of the "old man" after a person is saved. It refers to unredeemed humanness, the part of a believer that awaits future redemption at the time of his glorification (Rom. 8:23). Until then he has a redeemed self (cf. Gal. 2:20) living in an unredeemed humanness, and that creates great conflict.

Paul himself, like every other believer, faced that constant struggle with the flesh, as he confesses in his letter to the Romans.

> For I know that nothing good dwells in me, that is, in my flesh; for the willing is present in me, but the doing of the good is not. For the good that I want, I do not do; but I practice the very evil that I do not want. . . . I find then the principle that evil is present in me, the one who wants to do good. For I joyfully concur with the law of God in the inner man, but I see a different law in the members of my body, waging war against the law of my mind and making me a prisoner of the law of sin which is in my members. (Rom. 7:18–19, 21–23)

This specific usage of *sarx* ("flesh") is set among several other usages in the New Testament. The term occasionally refers to the physical body as well as to general humanness. It is also used to comprehensively describe the state of the unsaved, those who are "in the flesh" and thus totally under the control of sinful passions (Rom. 7:5). As such, "flesh" is generally used in a figurative, theological sense, referring to man's fallen nature, his unredeemed self. In the present text and others, "flesh" also relates to the moral and spiritual weakness and helplessness of human nature still clinging to redeemed souls, such as that mentioned by Paul in Romans 7 and quoted above (cf. Rom. 6:19). The "flesh" of Christians is their propensity to sin, their fallen humanness that awaits redemption, in which the new and holy creation dwells (cf. Gal. 2:20; 2 Cor. 5:17).

The flesh is that part of a believer that functions apart from and against the Spirit. It stands against the work of the Spirit in the believer's new heart. The unsaved person often regrets the sinful things he or she does because of guilt and/or painful consequences, but that person has no spiritual warfare going on within, because he has only a fleshly nature and is devoid of the Spirit. The sinful things the unsaved person does, though often disappointing and at times disgusting to him, are nevertheless consistent with his basic nature as an enemy of God (Rom. 5:10) and a child of His wrath (Eph. 2:3). He therefore has no real internal conflict beyond whatever conscience may remain in his sinful state.

The Spirit in Conflict with the Flesh

It is only in the lives of believers that the Spirit can fight against the flesh, because it is only in believers that the Spirit dwells. Only a believer can truthfully say, "I joyfully concur with the law of God in the inner man, but I see a different law in the members of my body, waging war against the law of my mind" (Rom. 7:22–23). Only in believers are the unredeemed flesh and the Spirit living in the redeemed self "in opposition to one another, so that [believers] may not do the things that [they] please" (Gal. 5:17).

Believers do not always do what they want to do. There are those moments in every Christian's experience when the wanting is present but the doing is not. The Spirit often halts what our flesh desires, and the flesh often overrides the will that comes from the Spirit. It is no surprise that this frustrating conflict led Paul to exclaim, "Wretched man that I am! Who will set me free from the body of this death?" (Rom. 7:24).

Although the Christian life is warfare, it is warfare in which victory is always possible. In His high priestly prayer Jesus spoke of the authority His Father had given Him "over all mankind" (lit., "all flesh," from *sarx*; John 17:2). Every believer has the indwelling power of God's own Spirit to do battle with his own weak and sinful flesh, in order that he may not do the things that please his flesh. In Romans 8:2, the apostle wrote: "the law of the Spirit . . . has set you free from the law of sin and of death." In other words, a third party is key to the conflict between the new creation and the flesh—the Holy Spirit. He energizes the new inner man for victory over his flesh.

As sons of God and servants of Jesus Christ, believers "are under obligation, not to the flesh, to live according to the flesh—for if [they] are living according to the flesh, [they] must die; but if by the Spirit [they] are putting to death the deeds of the body, [they] will live. For all who are being led by the Spirit of God, these are sons of God" (Rom. 8:12–14). "The Spirit also helps our weakness" when praying, Paul assures us; "for we do not know how to pray as we should, but the Spirit Himself intercedes for us with groanings too deep for words" (v. 26).

As already mentioned, the most effective way for a Christian to oppose the desires and deeds of the flesh is to starve them to death, to "make no provision for the flesh in regard to its lusts" (Rom. 13:14). The surest way to fall into a sin is to allow oneself to be in situations where there is temptation to it. On the other hand, the safest way to avoid a sin is to avoid situations that are likely to pose temptations to it. A believer should "consider the members of [his] earthly body as dead to immorality, impurity, passion, evil desire, and greed, which amounts to idolatry" (Col. 3:5). When our Lord told us to pray, "Do not lead us into temptation" (Matt. 6:13), He revealed that there is a part to sinful temptation that we must avoid.

A believer who is not actively involved in resisting evil and obviously seeking to do good is not being led by the Spirit, no matter how much he may think he is "surrendered." The faithful believer is not an observer but "a good soldier of Christ Jesus" who is engaged in the "active service" of his Lord (2 Tim. 2:23–4).

The faithful believer is also compared to an athlete. Paul commands Christians to "run in such a way that [they] may win" and to exercise self-control. He speaks of himself as running "in such a way, as not without aim," of boxing "in such a way, as not beating the air," and of buffeting his body to make it his slave (1 Cor. 9:24–27).

True Balance for the Battle

A believer can accomplish nothing for the Lord in his own power, but, on the other hand, the Spirit can accomplish little through a believer apart from the believer's submission and commitment. The opposite extreme of quietism is traditionally labelled "pietism," in which a believer legalistically strives in his own power to do everything the Lord commands of him. There the emphasis is overbalanced on the side of discipline, self-effort, and personal diligence.

The apostle Peter beautifully explains the true balance of the Christian life. According to "His divine power [God] has granted to us everything pertaining to life and godliness, through the true knowledge of Him who called us by His own glory and excellence. For by these He has granted to us His precious and magnificent promises, so that by them you may become partakers of the divine nature, having escaped the corruption that is in the world by lust" (2 Peter 1:3–4). That is God's commitment, in the power of which the believer's commitment should be to apply all diligence and in faith to supply moral excellence, knowledge, self-control, perseverance, and godliness (vv. 5–6).

It is not a matter of "All of Him and none of us," as the popular saying has it; and it is certainly not a matter of all of us and none of Him. It is the balance of our yieldedness and commitment with the Spirit's guidance and power. "Work out your salvation with fear and trembling," Paul says; "for it is God who is at work in you, both to will and to work for His good pleasure" (Phil. 2:12–13). The mystery of this perfect and paradoxical balance cannot be fully understood or explained, but it can be fully experienced.

As a repeated warning to believers who were being influenced by the Judaizers, Paul added, "But if you are led by the Spirit, you are not under the Law" (Gal. 5:18). To live "under the Law" is to live by the flesh, even when one is not actually committing sin, because that is the only avenue available to the legalist. The flesh is powerless to fulfill the Law, and the Law is powerless to conquer the flesh.

In his *Pilgrim's Progress,* John Bunyan describes Interpreter's house, which Pilgrim entered during the course of his journey to the Celestial City. The parlor of the house was completely covered with dust, and when a man took a broom and started to sweep, he and the others in the room began to choke from the great clouds of dust that were stirred up. The more vigorously he swept, the more suffocating the dust became. Then Interpreter ordered a maid to sprinkle the room with water, with which the dust was quickly washed away. Interpreter explained to Pilgrim that the parlor represented the heart of an unsaved man, that the dust was original sin, the man with the broom was the law, and the maid with the water was the gospel. His point was that all the law can do with sin is to stir it up. Only the gospel of Jesus Christ can wash it away.

"The power of sin is the law," Paul declares; "but thanks be to God, who gives us the victory through our Lord Jesus Christ" (1 Cor. 15:56–57).

To be led by the Spirit is the same as walking by Him (Gal. 5:16, 25) but carries additional emphasis on His leadership. We do not walk along with Him as an equal, but follow His leading as our sovereign, divine Guide. "For all who are being led by the Spirit of God, these are sons of God," Paul says (Rom. 8:14). The converse is also true: Those who are sons of God are led by the Spirit of God. Believers do not need to pray for the Spirit's leading, because He is already doing that. They need to seek for willingness and obedience to follow His leading.

When Christ enters a person's life, the Holy Spirit enters simultaneously (cf. Rom. 8:9). And the moment He enters He begins to lead God's newborn child in the way of freedom (Gal. 5:1), holiness (5:16), truth (John 16:13–15), fruitfulness (Gal. 5:22–23), access to God in prayer (Eph. 2:18), assurance (Rom. 8:16), witnessing (Acts 1:8), and submissive joy (Eph. 5:18–21).

No wonder Paul rejoiced that "what the Law could not do, weak as it was through the flesh, God did: sending His own Son in the likeness of sinful flesh and as an offering for sin, He condemned sin in the flesh, so that the requirement of the Law might be fulfilled in us, who do not walk according to the flesh but according to the Spirit" (Rom. 8:3–4).

THE CONTRAST

Now the deeds of the flesh are evident, which are: immorality, impurity, sensuality, idolatry, sorcery, enmities, strife, jealousy, outbursts of anger, disputes, dissensions, factions, envying, drunkenness, carousing, and things like these, of which I forewarn you, just as I have forewarned you, that those who practice such things will not inherit the kingdom of God. But the fruit of the Spirit is love, joy, peace, patience, kindness, goodness,

faithfulness, gentleness, self-control; against such things there is no law. (5:19–23)

As a motivation to godly living, Paul places the products of living in the flesh side by side with the products of living by the Spirit. The sins of the first list are the ugly and repulsive results of evil desire, whereas the virtues of the second are the beautiful and attractive results of walking by the Spirit. Neither list is exhaustive but only suggestive (see v. 21, "things like these"; and v. 23, "such things") of things that first of all were pertinent to the Galatian church and, second, are pertinent to all believers.

The Deeds of the Flesh

Now the deeds of the flesh are evident, which are: immorality, impurity, sensuality, idolatry, sorcery, enmities, strife, jealousy, outbursts of anger, disputes, dissensions, factions, envying, drunkenness, carousing, and things like these, of which I forewarn you, just as I have forewarned you, that those who practice such things will not inherit the kingdom of God. (5:19–21)

"The deeds of the flesh" reflect the sinful desires of unredeemed humanness, which are in spiritual warfare against the desires of the Spirit (vv. 16–17; cf. 24). These deeds are so evident that Paul mentions them primarily by way of a reminder.

Jesus made clear that man's basic problem is not with what is outside of him but with what is within him. "That which proceeds out of the man, that is what defiles the man. For from within, out of the heart of men, proceed the evil thoughts, fornications, thefts, murders, adulteries, deeds of coveting and wickedness, as well as deceit, sensuality, envy, slander, pride and foolishness. All these evil things proceed from within and defile the man" (Mark 7:20–23).

Jesus' list is much like Paul's, and in both passages the point is made that these evils originate from within man himself, not from Satan or the world outside. In that brief account Jesus mentions three times that the sins come from within man himself, and Paul identifies his list of sins as "deeds of the flesh," that is, works produced by man's own unregenerate nature.

There are only two possible views of man's nature: he is seen either as basically good or basically evil. The humanistic view is that he is born morally good, or at least morally neutral. The Bible, however, maintains the opposite, that man is inherently corrupt and depraved in every aspect of his being. Consequently, although man's environment is never perfect and often has a detrimental effect on him, that is never his worst problem. It is primarily man who pollutes the environment, not the environment that pollutes him.

That is why better housing, transportation, education, jobs, income, medical care, and all other such things—desirable as they may be—can do nothing to solve man's basic problem, which is sin inside of him. No outward benefit can improve him inwardly. Instead, better outward conditions offer better and more sophisticated opportunities to do evil and for those very benefits themselves to be corrupted by the people they are designed to help.

Though the sins that Paul lists here (cf. Rom. 1:29–31; 2 Cor. 12:20–21) are natural characteristics of unredeemed mankind, not every person manifests all of the sins or manifests them to the same degree. However, every person possesses "the flesh," which is sinful and will therefore be manifested in sinful behavior, whatever the particular forms of it may be. These are normal and continual behaviors for unbelievers in their course of life in the flesh, but are abnormal and interruptive behavior in the lives of Christians, who live in the Spirit. A Christian can walk in the Spirit and avoid them all, or he can give in to the flesh and fall victim to any of them.

Paul's list of the deeds of the flesh encompasses three general areas: sex, religion, and human relationships.

DEFILEMENT THROUGH SEXUAL SIN

The first group of sins relates to man's defilement in the area of sex. "Immorality" is from the Greek *porneia*, from which is derived the English *pornography*. The term has a broad meaning, referring to all illicit sexual activity—especially, but not limited to, adultery, fornication, homosexuality, bestiality, and prostitution. In 1 Corinthians 5:1, Paul uses the term to refer to a form of incest (sexual relationships of a man with his mother or stepmother) that even the pagans did not practice. In the next two chapters (6:13, 18; 7:2; cf. Eph. 5:3; 1 Thess. 4:3) he uses the same word to represent sexual sin in general.

"Impurity" is from *akatharsia*, which literally means "unclean" and was used medically to refer to an infected, oozing wound. It is the negative form of *katharsia*, which means "clean" and is the word from which we get *catharsis*, a cleansing. In Scripture the term is used of both moral and ceremonial uncleanness, any impurity that prevents a person from approaching God.

"Sensuality" is from *aselgeia*, which originally referred to any excess or lack of restraint but came to be associated primarily with sexual excess. It is unrestrained sexual indulgence, such as has become so common in the modern Western world. It refers to uninhibited sexual indulgence without shame and without concern for what others think or how they may be affected (or infected).

DEFILEMENT BY MAN-MADE RELIGION

The second group of sins, specifically idolatry and sorcery, relates to man-made religion, which is as much a product of the flesh as are sexual sins. The deeds of the flesh not only defile men themselves but also their relationship to God. All human religion is based on self-effort, on man's sinful insistence that he can make himself acceptable to his humanly-conceived God by his own merits. Consequently, human religion is the implacable enemy of divine grace and therefore of the gospel.

"Idolatry" is the obvious sin of worshiping man-made images of whatever sort. "Sorcery" is from the Greek *pharmakeia*, from which we get *pharmacy* and *pharmaceutical*. It was originally used of medicines in general but came to be used primarily of mood— and mind—altering drugs similar to those that create so much havoc in our own day. Many ancient religious ceremonies involved occult practices in which drugs were used to induce supposed communication with deities, and *pharmakeia* thereby came to be closely related to witchcraft and magic. Aristotle and other ancient Greek writers used the word as a synonym for witchcraft and black magic, because drugs were so commonly used in their practice.

DEFILEMENT OF HUMAN RELATIONSHIPS

The third group of sins relates to human relationships, which are defiled by these specific sins as well as by many others.

"Enmities" is in the plural and refers to hateful attitudes, which result in strife among individuals, including bitter conflicts. Wrong attitudes invariably bring wrong actions.

"Jealousy" is a form of anger and hateful resentment caused by coveting for oneself what belongs to someone else. "Outbursts of anger" are sudden, unrestrained expressions of hostility toward others, often with little or no provocation or justification. It is the all-too-common sin of unbridled temper. Although "jealousy" does not necessarily result in outbursts of anger in the way that enmities result in strife, the first sin in each case refers to attitude or motive and the second to action.

"Disputes, dissensions, factions, [and] envying" are more particular and ongoing expressions of the general sins that precede them in this list. They represent animosities between individuals and groups that sometimes continue to fester and grow long after the original cause of conflict has passed. From the feuds of old-time mountain clans that lasted for generations to national hostilities that last for centuries, these sins can become an established and destructive way of life.

"Drunkenness" and "carousing" probably had special reference to the orgies that so often characterized the pagan worship ceremonies that many of the Gentile converts of Galatia had once participated in. In a more general and universal sense, however, they refer to becoming drunk under any circumstance and to all rowdy, boisterous, and crude behavior.

As already observed, "and things like these" indicates that Paul's list of deeds of the flesh is only representative and not exhaustive. Nor were these sins ones that Galatian believers had only recently been tempted by or fallen into. "I forewarn you" again, Paul says, "just as I have forewarned you" in the past. These appear to have been sins that were dominant in the culture and by which the Galatians were still being tempted.

A WARNING TO "THOSE WHO PRACTICE SUCH THINGS"

The high point of the apostle's forewarning is sobering: "those who practice such things will not inherit the kingdom of God."

Because the list of sins is so all-encompassing and the warning so severe, this passage has caused many believers to doubt their salvation. Such fears have been compounded by the unfortunate rendering of the King James version: "they which do such things." "Who hasn't done some of those things?" people wonder. "What Christian can claim he has not committed a single one of those sins since he was saved? Who could possibly enter the kingdom of God if committing just one of those sins keeps him out?"

The key word in Paul's warning is "practice," which translates a present active participle of *prassō*, indicating durative, ongoing action. It is the continual, habitual practice of such things that marks a person as unregenerate and therefore barred from entrance into the kingdom of God. Scripture always assesses a person's character on the basis of his common, habitual actions, not his occasional ones. People who habitually indulge in sin show themselves to be enemies of God, whereas those who habitually do good show themselves to be His children. The unregenerate person occasionally does humanly good things, and the regenerate person occasionally falls into sin. But the basic character of the unregenerate is to practice the evil deeds of the flesh and of the regenerate person to bear the good fruit of the Spirit. This is the heart of John's teaching in 1 John 3:4–10.

> Everyone who practices sin also practices lawlessness; and sin is lawlessness. You know that He appeared in order to take away sins; and in Him there is no sin. No one who abides in Him sins; no one who sins has seen Him or knows Him. Little children, make sure no one deceive you; the one who practices righteousness is righteous, just as He is righteous; the one who practices sin is of the devil; for the devil has sinned from the beginning. The Son of God appeared for

this purpose, to destroy the works of the devil. No one who is born of God practices sin, because His seed abides in him; and he cannot sin, because he is born of God. By this the children of God and the children of the devil are obvious: anyone who does not practice righteousness is not of God, nor the one who does not love his brother.

Paul makes a similar statement in 1 Corinthians 6:9–10, "Or do you not know that the unrighteous will not inherit the kingdom of God? Do not be deceived; neither fornicators, nor idolaters, nor adulterers, nor effeminate, nor homosexuals, nor thieves, nor the covetous, nor drunkards, nor revilers, nor swindlers, will inherit the kingdom of God." He then makes clear that such things are no longer the practice of believers: "Such were some of you; but you were washed, but you were sanctified, but you were justified in the name of the Lord Jesus Christ and in the Spirit of our God" (v. 11).

Even though they are not habitually doing such evils, Paul calls on saints to walk in the Spirit so that they do not even do them occasionally.

The Fruit of the Spirit

But the fruit of the Spirit is love, joy, peace, patience, kindness, goodness, faithfulness, gentleness, self-control; against such things there is no law. (5:22–23)

Contrasted with the deeds of the flesh is the fruit of the Spirit. The deeds of the flesh are done by a person's own efforts, whether he is saved or unsaved. The fruit of the Spirit, on the other hand, is produced *by* God's own Spirit and only in the lives of those who belong to Him through faith in Jesus Christ.

The spiritual behavior of walking by the Spirit (v. 16) has the "negative" effect of causing the believer to put away the habitual, ongoing evil deeds of the flesh; its positive effect is to cause the Christian to bear the good fruit produced by the Spirit.

The first contrast between the deeds of the flesh and the fruit of the Spirit is that the products of the flesh are plural, whereas the product of the Spirit is singular. Although Paul does not mention the truth here, there is also a contrast between the degrees to which the deeds and the fruit are produced. A given person may habitually practice only one or two, or perhaps a half dozen, of the sins Paul mentions here. But it would be practically impossible for one person to be habitually active in all of them. The fruit of the Spirit, on the other hand, is always produced completely in every believer, no matter how faintly evidenced its various manifestations may be.

The Bible has much to say about fruit, which is mentioned some 106 times in the Old Testament and seventy times in the New. Even under the covenant of law, a believer produced good fruit only by God's power, not his own. "From Me comes your fruit," the Lord declared to ancient Israel (Hos. 14:8).

In the New Testament such things as praise of the Lord (Heb. 13:15), winning converts to Christ (1 Cor. 16:15), and godly work in general (Col. 1:10) are spoken of as spiritual fruit produced through believers. But such *action* fruit must come from *attitude* fruit, and that is the kind of fruit Paul focuses on in Galatians 5:22-23. If those attitudes are characteristic of a believer's life, the fruit of active good works will inevitably follow.

SOME FRUIT VERSUS MUCH FRUIT

The Spirit never fails to produce some fruit in a believer's life, but the Lord desires "much fruit" (John 15:8). As an unredeemed person, possessing only a fallen, sinful nature will inevitably manifest that nature in "the deeds of the flesh" (v. 19), so a believer, possessing a redeemed new nature will inevitably manifest that new nature in the fruit of the Spirit. But it is always possible for the believer to bear and manifest more fruit if he is receptive to the Spirit.

The Spirit's provision of fruit might be compared to a man standing on a ladder in an orchard, picking the fruit and dropping it into a basket held by a helper below. No matter how much fruit is picked and dropped, the helper will not receive any unless he is standing under the ladder with his basket ready.

The fruit of the Spirit is the outward indicator of salvation. A believer's sonship to God and citizenship in His kingdom (cf. v. 21) are manifested by the fruit the Spirit produces in his life. "You will know [men and women] by their fruits," Jesus said. "Grapes are not gathered from thorn bushes nor figs from thistles, are they? So every good tree bears good fruit, but the bad tree bears bad fruit. A good tree cannot produce bad fruit, nor can a bad tree produce good fruit" (Matt. 7:16–18).

In verses 22–23 Paul lists nine representative characteristics of the godly fruit produced by the Holy Spirit in a believer's life. Although many attempts have been made to categorize these nine virtues in various groupings, most such schemes seem artificial and irrelevant. Whether or not satisfactory classifications of them can be made, it is important to remember that these are multiple characteristics of but one fruit and are therefore inextricably related to one another. They are not produced nor can they be manifested in isolation from each other.

Rather paradoxically, all of the nine manifestations of the fruit of the Spirit are also *commanded* of believers in the New Testament. Also in every case, Jesus can be seen to be the supreme example and the Holy Spirit to be the source.

LOVE

The first characteristic of spiritual fruit is love, the supreme virtue of Christian living (1 Cor. 13:13). Some commentators insist that in this context love is a synonym for fruit and therefore encompasses the other characteristics in the list. In any case, love is clearly dominant. As Paul has just declared, "the whole Law is fulfilled in one word, in the statement, 'You shall love your neighbor as yourself'" (Gal. 5:14; cf. Rom. 13:10).

Agapē love is the form of love that most reflects personal choice, referring not simply to pleasant emotions or good feelings but to willing, self-giving service. "God demonstrates His own love toward us, in that while we were yet sinners, Christ died for us" (Rom. 5:8). In the same way, the most extreme sacrificial choice a loving person can make is to "lay down his life for his friends" (John 15:13). The apostle John expresses those two truths together in his first letter: "We know love by this, that He laid down His life for us; and we ought to lay down our lives for the brethren" (1 John 3:16). But love is tested long before it is called on to offer that supreme sacrifice. As John goes on to say, "Whoever has the world's goods, and sees his brother in need and closes his heart against him, how does the love of God abide in him?" (v. 17). A person who thinks his love is great enough to sacrifice his life for fellow believers but who fails to help them when they have less extreme needs is simply fooling himself.

True *agapē* love is a sure mark of salvation. "We know that we have passed out of death into life," John writes, "because we love the brethren. . . . Everyone who loves is born of God and knows God" (1 John 3:14; 4:7). By the same token, as John repeatedly makes clear throughout the same letter, having a habitually unloving spirit toward fellow Christians is reason for a person to question his salvation (see e.g., 2:9, 11; 3:15; 4:8, 20).

Jesus Christ is the supreme example of this supreme virtue. It was not only the Father's love but also His own love that led Jesus to lay down His life for us, demonstrating with His own self-sacrifice the love that gives its life for its friends. And before He made the ultimate sacrifice, He demonstrated the same self-giving love in many lesser ways. As Jesus saw Mary and the others weeping because of Lazarus's death, He, too, wept (John 11:33–35). He did not grieve for the fact that Lazarus had died, because He purposely delayed coming to Bethany until His dear friend was dead, in order to demonstrate His power to raise him from the grave. Jesus wept because of the great evil, destruction, and human misery caused by sin, whose final wages is always death (Rom. 6:23).

For believers, love is not an option but a command. "Walk in love," Paul declared, "just as Christ also loved you and gave Himself up for us, an offering and a sacrifice to God as a fragrant aroma" (Eph. 5:2). Yet the command cannot be fulfilled apart from the Holy Spirit, the source of this and all the other manifestations of spiritual fruit. "The love of God has been poured out within our hearts through the Holy Spirit who was given to us," Paul explained to Roman believers (Rom. 5:5), and it was for such "love in the Spirit" that he gave thanks for the believers in Colossae (Col. 1:8).

JOY

The second manifestation of the fruit of the Spirit is joy. *Chara* (joy) is used some seventy times in the New Testament, always to signify a feeling of happiness that is based on spiritual realities. Joy is the deep-down sense of well-being that abides in the heart of the person who knows all is well between himself and the Lord.

It is not an experience that comes from favorable circumstances or even a human emotion that is divinely stimulated. It is God's gift to believers. As Nehemiah declared, "The joy of the Lord is your strength" (Neh. 8:10). Joy is a part of God's own nature and the Holy Spirit that He manifests in His children.

Joy not only does not come from favorable human circumstances but is sometimes greatest when those circumstances are the most painful and severe. Shortly before His arrest and crucifixion, Jesus told His disciples, "Truly, truly, I say to you, that you will weep and lament, but the world will rejoice; you will grieve, but your grief will be turned to joy" (John 16:20). To illustrate that truth Jesus compared divine joy to a woman in childbirth. "She has pain, because her hour has come; but when she gives birth to the child, she no longer remembers the anguish because of the joy that a child has been born into the world. Therefore you too have grief now; but I will see you again, and your heart will rejoice, and no one will take your joy away from you" (vv. 21–22).

God's joy is full, complete in every way. Nothing human or circumstantial can add to it or detract from it. But it is not fulfilled in a believer's life except through reliance on and obedience to the Lord. "Ask and you will receive," Jesus went on to explain, "so that your joy may be made full" (John 16:24). One of John's motivations in writing his first epistle was that his joy might "be made complete" (1 John 1:4).

Jesus Himself is again our supreme example. He was "a man of sorrows, and acquainted with grief" (Isa. 53:3; cf. Luke 18:31–33), but, just as He had promised for His disciples, His sorrow was turned into joy. "For the joy set before Him [He] endured the cross, despising the shame, and has sat down at the right hand of the throne of God" (Heb. 12:2). Despite the misunderstanding,

THE BELIEVER'S WALK WITH CHRIST

the rejection, the hatred, and the pain He endured from men while incarnate among them, the Lord never lost His joy in the relationship He had with His Father. And that joy He gives to each of His followers.

Speaking of how we feel about the Lord Jesus Christ, Peter wrote, "Though you have not seen Him, you love Him, and though you do not see Him now, but believe in Him, you greatly rejoice with joy inexpressible and full of glory" (1 Peter 1:8). Joy is the inevitable overflow of receiving Jesus Christ as Savior and of the believer's knowing His continuing presence.

Although joy is a gift of God through His Spirit to those who belong to Christ, it is also commanded of them "Rejoice in the Lord always; again I will say, rejoice!" Paul commands (Phil. 4:4; cf. 3:1). Because joy comes as a gift from Him, the command obviously is not for believers to manufacture or try to imitate it. The command is to gratefully accept and revel in this great blessing they already possess. "For the kingdom of God is not eating and drinking, but righteousness and peace and joy in the Holy Spirit" (Rom. 14:17).

PEACE

If joy speaks of the exhilaration of heart that comes from being right with God, then "peace" (*eirēnē*) refers to the tranquility of mind that comes from that saving relationship. The verb form has to do with binding together and is reflected in the modern expression "having it all together." Everything is in place and as it ought to be.

Like joy, peace has no relationship to circumstances. Christians know "that God causes all things to work together for good to those who love God, to those who are called according to His purpose" (Rom. 8:28). Because God is in control of all aspects of a believer's life, how his circumstances may appear from a human perspective makes no ultimate difference. That is why Jesus could say without qualification to those who trust in Him, "Do not let your heart be troubled" (John 14:1). There is absolutely no reason for a believer to be anxious or afraid.

Jesus was the Prince of Peace, both in the sense that He was supremely peaceful Himself and in the sense that He dispenses His peace to those who are His. Even when He confronted Satan face-to-face in the wilderness, Jesus had perfect peace, knowing His heavenly Father was continually with Him and would supply His every need (Matt. 4:1–11). It is His own peace that He bequeaths to His disciples: "Peace I leave with you; My peace I give to you; not as the world gives do I give to you" (John 14:27).

"The things you have learned and received and heard and seen in me, practice these things," Paul said; "and the God of peace will be with you" (Phil. 4:9). Because they have the God of peace in their hearts, believers need "be anxious for nothing," having "the peace of God, which surpasses all comprehension [to] guard [their] hearts and [their] minds in Christ Jesus" (vv. 6–7).

PATIENCE

The Greek word for patience, *makrothumia,* has to do with tolerance and longsuffering that endure injuries inflicted by others, the calm willingness to accept situations that are irritating or painful.

God Himself is "slow to anger" (Ps. 86:15) and expects His children to be the same. Just as believers should never "think lightly of the riches of [God's own] kindness and tolerance and patience" (Rom. 2:4), they should themselves manifest those attributes of their heavenly Father.

In the last days, arrogant unbelievers will taunt Christians by asking, "Where is the promise of [Christ's] coming? For ever since the fathers fell asleep, all continues just as it was from the beginning of creation" (2 Peter 3:4). In their sin-darkened minds unbelievers will fail to see that, just as in the days of Noah, when God patiently delayed the Flood in order to give men more time to repent (1 Peter 3:20), it is also because of His merciful patience that He forestalls Christ's second coming and the accompanying judgment on unbelievers, "not wishing for any to perish but for all to come to repentance" (2 Peter 3:9).

Paul confessed that, as the foremost of sinners, he found mercy in God's sight "so that in [him] as the foremost, Jesus Christ might demonstrate His perfect patience as an example for those who would believe in Him for eternal life" (1 Tim. 1:15–16).

Believers are commanded to emulate their Lord's patience. "As those who have been chosen of God, holy and beloved," they are to "put on a heart of . . . patience" (Col. 3:12), especially with fellow believers, "showing tolerance for one another in love" (Eph. 4:2). Like Timothy, all Christian teachers and leaders are to minister "with great patience" (2 Tim. 4:2).

KINDNESS

Chrēstotēs ("kindness") relates to tender concern for others. It has nothing to do with weakness or lack of conviction but is the genuine desire of a believer to treat others gently, just as the Lord treats him. Paul reminded the Thessalonians that, even though he was an apostle, he "proved to be gentle among [them], as a nursing mother tenderly cares for her own children" (1 Thess. 2:6–7).

Jesus' kindness is the believer's example. When "some children were brought to Him so that He might lay His hands on them and pray; and the disciples rebuked them. . . . Jesus said, 'Let the children alone, and do not hinder them from coming to Me; for the kingdom of heaven belongs to such as these'" (Matt. 19:13–14). On another occasion He said, "Come to Me, all who are weary and heavy-laden, and I will give you rest. Take My yoke upon you and learn from Me, for I am gentle and humble in heart; and you will find rest for your souls" (Matt. 11:28–29).

Just as their Lord is kind, His servants are commanded not to "be quarrelsome, but [to] be kind to all" (2 Tim. 2:24). And just as He does with all the other manifestations of His divine fruit, the Holy Spirit gives God's children kindness (2 Cor. 6:6).

GOODNESS

Agathos ("goodness") has to do with moral and spiritual excellence that is known by its sweetness and active kindness. Paul helped define this virtue when he observed that "one will hardly die for a righteous man; though perhaps for the good man someone would dare even to die" (Rom. 5:7). A Christian can be morally upright but still not manifest the grace of goodness. He may be admired and respected for his high moral standards and might even have a friend who would risk his life for him. But the upright person who also has goodness is much more likely to have self-sacrificing friends.

Joseph was such a righteous and good man. When he learned that Mary was pregnant but did not yet know it was by the Holy Spirit, "being a righteous man" he could not bring himself to marry her, assuming she had been unfaithful. But being also a good man, he could not bear the thought of disgracing his beloved Mary and therefore "planned to send her away secretly" (Matt. 1:19).

David had a deep understanding of God's goodness, as he

repeatedly reveals in his psalms. "Surely goodness and lovingkindness will follow me all the days of my life, and I will dwell in the house of the Lord forever," he rejoiced (Ps. 23:6). He confessed that he would, in fact, "have despaired unless [he] had believed that [he] would see the goodness of the Lord in the land of the living" (Ps. 27:13).

As with every grace the Spirit provides, believers are commanded to exemplify goodness. Later in the letter Paul exhorts, "While we have opportunity, let us do good to all people, and especially to those who are of the household of the faith" (Gal. 6:10). "To this end also we pray for you always," he wrote to the Thessalonians, "that our God will count you worthy of your calling, and fulfill every desire for goodness and the work of faith with power" (2 Thess. 1:11).

FAITHFULNESS

Pistis ("faithfulness") pertains to loyalty and trustworthiness. The "servants of Christ and stewards of the mysteries of God" are to be like their Lord in being "found trustworthy" (1 Cor. 4:1–2). "Be faithful unto death, and I will give you the crown of life," the Lord assures His followers (Rev. 2:10).

The Lord Jesus was faithful to the point that He "emptied Himself, taking the form of a bond-servant, . . . being made in the likeness of men. [Then] He humbled Himself by becoming obedient to the point of death, even death on a cross." And because of the Son's faithfulness, the Father "highly exalted Him, and bestowed on Him the name which is above every name" (Phil. 2:7–9).

And as He was faithful when He came to earth the first time, He will be faithful to come again "in just the same way as you have watched Him go into heaven" (Acts 1:11). "Faithful is He who calls you," Paul said, "and He also will bring it to pass" (1 Thess. 5:24).

GENTLENESS

The Greek word for "gentleness" is *prautēs,* which includes the idea of gentleness but is usually better translated *meekness.* In his helpful volume *Synonyms of the New Testament,* R. C. Trench writes that *prautēs* does not consist in a person's "outward behavior only; nor yet in his relations to his fellow-men; as little as in his mere natural disposition. Rather it is an inwrought grace of the soul; and the exercises of it are first and chiefly towards God. It is that temper of spirit in which we accept His dealings with us as good, and therefore without disputing or resisting."[2] It is that humble and gentle attitude that is patiently submissive in every offense, while being free of any desire for revenge or retribution.

Of the nine characteristics of the fruit of the Spirit, this one and the one following do not apply to God as God the Father. The Old Testament never refers to God as being meek, and in the New Testament only the Son is spoken of as meek, and that only in His incarnation.

In the New Testament *prautēs* is used to describe three attitudes: submissiveness to the will of God (Col. 3:12), teachableness (James 1:21), and consideration of others (Eph. 4:2).

Although He was God, while He lived on earth as the Son of Man, Jesus was "gentle [*prautēs*] and humble in heart" (Matt. 11:29; cf. 21:5; 2 Cor. 10:1). Like their Lord, believers are to actively pursue meekness and gentleness (1 Tim. 6:11) and to wear them like a garment (Col. 3:12).

SELF-CONTROL

Enkrateia, the Greek word used for "self-control," has reference to restraining passions and appetites. As with meekness, however, this grace does not apply to God, who obviously does not need to restrain Himself. "For I, the Lord, do not change," He informs us (Mal. 3:6). In His eternal being, the Lord "Jesus Christ is the same yesterday and today and forever" (Heb. 13:8). Perfect holiness possesses perfect control.

But in His incarnation Christ was the epitome of self-control. He was never tempted or tricked into doing or saying anything that was not consistent with His Father's will and His own divine nature. Again like Jesus, believers should "exercise self-control in all things" (1 Cor. 9:25; cf. 7:9), "applying all diligence, in [their] faith [to] supply . . . self-control" (2 Pet. 1:5–6).

"SUCH THINGS" ARE NEVER HARMFUL

"Against such things there is no law," Paul writes. Even unbelievers do not make laws against such things as those that the fruit of the Spirit produces. The world does not make laws against such behavior, but generally prizes it. Even if some consider "such things" to be signs of weakness, they cannot escape recognizing that they are never harmful.

There is certainly no law of God "against such things," because those are the very virtues He wants all men and women to have and that He gives to them when they put their trust in Jesus Christ as Lord and Savior. "For if these qualities are yours and are increasing," Peter explains in regard to a similar list of virtues, "they render you neither useless nor unfruitful in the true knowledge of our Lord Jesus Christ" (2 Pet. 1:8).

The believer who walks in the Spirit and manifests His fruit does not need a system of law to produce the right attitudes and behavior—they rise from within him.

The Conquest

Now those who belong to Christ Jesus have crucified the flesh with its passions and desires. If we live by the Spirit, let us also walk by the Spirit. (5:24–25)

All persons who belong to Christ Jesus by faith in Him and His perfect saving work "have crucified the flesh with its passions and desires." "Have crucified the flesh" is a strategic statement to grasp, because crucifixion was a means of execution. All but four uses of the term in the New Testament refer to the death of Jesus Christ on the cross. Three of the exceptions help in understanding the fourth, which is in the present text.

The first of the three is in the book of Romans, where Paul affirms that at the time of our justification, "our old self was crucified with [Christ]" (6:6). The other two are in Galatians, one before and one after the present text. The apostle says, "I have been crucified with Christ" (2:20), and, near the end of the epistle, asserts that "the world has been crucified to me" (6:14).

In each of those three passages, "crucified" is simply a vivid and dramatic way to say "killed," or "executed." In the first two passages Paul is teaching that at salvation his old, sinful, unregenerate self was executed and he was born a new man in Christ Jesus. In the third passage he is saying that the world has been executed and is now dead to him so that it is no longer his master, holding him in bondage. He is therefore now free to serve the Lord.

Obviously, in none of those passages does Paul mean to imply that the crucifixion analogy carries the idea of total death, in which all influence ceases. Sin was still a reality in his life, and so was the temptation of the world. But there was a sense in which the power of the old self and of the world was broken. Those influences no longer dominated him.

In the text of Galatians 5:24, Paul is saying that "the flesh" has been executed. But how could that be in light of what he has just said in this chapter about believers having a constant war with the ever-present flesh? In what sense is the flesh killed at conversion?

It cannot be in the actual, complete, present sense or it would contradict the reality of the continual spiritual conflict with the flesh indicated here and in Romans 7:14–25. And it cannot be that Paul has some future sense in mind or he would have used a future verb form, saying, "shall crucify the flesh," referring to the time of glorification.

The best understanding is to see "have crucified" as an allusion to the cross of Jesus Christ, which, as a past event, fits the aorist tense used here by Paul. It looks back to the cross, the time at which the death of the flesh was actually accomplished. Yet, because we are still alive on the earth and still possess our humanness, we have not yet entered into the future fullness of that past event.

Meanwhile, "the flesh with its passions [or affections] and desires" is dead in the sense of no longer reigning over us or of holding us in inescapable bondage. Like a chicken with its head cut off, the flesh has been dealt a death blow, although it continues to flop around the barnyard of earth until the last nerve is stilled.

Because the flesh is defeated forever, and we now live in the realm where Christ reigns over us by His Spirit, we should live according to the Spirit and not the flesh.

Because believers have new life in Jesus Christ, they should also have a new *way* of life. If we live by the Spirit—and we do—Paul says, "let us also walk by the Spirit"—as we must.

Chapter 5

———∞———

WALKING IN OBEDIENCE

1 John 2:3–6

By this we know that we have come to know Him, if we keep His commandments. The one who says, "I have come to know Him," and does not keep His commandments, is a liar, and the truth is not in him; but whoever keeps His word, in him the love of God has truly been perfected. By this we know that we are in Him: the one who says he abides in Him ought himself to walk in the same manner as He walked. (2:3–6)

Assurance," wrote the seventeenth-century English Puritan Thomas Brooks, "is a reflex act of a gracious soul, whereby he clearly and evidently sees himself in a gracious, blessed, and happy state; it is a sensible feeling, and an experimental [experiential] discerning of a man's being in a state of grace."[1]

Earlier Brooks had compared assurance to an ark: "Assurance is a believer's ark, where he sits, Noah-like, quiet and still in the midst of all distractions and destructions, commotions and confusions."[2]

Assurance causes believers to rejoice with the hymn writer, "Blessed assurance, Jesus is mine! O what a foretaste of glory divine!" To possess assurance is, in a sense, to experience heaven on earth.

THE STRUGGLE FOR ASSURANCE

But sadly, as Brooks goes on to lament, assurance "is a pearl that most want, a crown that few wear. . . . Little well-grounded assurance . . . is to be found among most Christians. Most Christians live between fears and hopes, and hang, as it were, between heaven and hell, sometimes they hope that their state is good, at other times they fear that their state is bad."[3]

Assurance is not only a privilege, it is also a birthright that Christians possess as members of the body of Christ (Rom. 5:1; 8:16; cf. Ps. 4:3; John 10:27–29; Phil. 1:6; 1 Thess. 1:4). Not having it, on the other hand, and thereby doubting one's salvation, produces uncertainty and fear that brings misery and despair.

Though the assurance of salvation is part of redemption and vital to joy and comfort, God's Word teaches that it is possible to forfeit it, unless one pursues it. The apostle Peter wrote, "Therefore, brethren, be all the more diligent to make certain about His calling and choosing you" (2 Peter 1:10; cf. Heb. 10:22). Peter revealed that this certainty comes to those who pursue all the features of holiness with increasing diligence (vv. 5–8).

Yet, in spite of such biblical mandates, many in contemporary Christianity simply ignore the biblical understanding of assurance. Teachers frequently assure them that if they have repeated a certain prayer, gone forward at an evangelistic rally, made a profession of faith, given mental assent to the gospel, or even been baptized, they are definitely saved and should never question their salvation. Such people do not want to examine themselves as the Bible teaches

(2 Cor. 13:5), because to do so, they reason, might damage their fragile self-esteem or make them guilty of doubting God. As a result, the entire subject of assurance is often de-emphasized or ignored altogether.

But that has not always been the case. Throughout church history, the personal assurance of salvation has been a major issue.[4] On the one hand, Roman Catholicism has always adamantly denied the possibility of assurance. This perspective stems from the Catholic heresy that justification is a joint effort between God and sinners. God will always do His part, but the sinner might not do his or her part; thus no one can be assured of salvation in this life. In the words of the Council of Trent (1545–63), any "believer's assurance of the pardon of his sins is a vain and ungodly confidence."[5] Cardinal Roberto Bellarmine, a Jesuit theologian of that era, once stated that assurance is "a prime error of heretics."[6] In other words, according to Catholicism, no one can truly know whether he or she has received salvation until the afterlife—and to think one can is heretical.

When the sixteenth-century Protestant Reformers recovered the true gospel from Rome and reasserted the biblical doctrine of salvation, they also accurately expounded the issue of assurance. Contrary to Roman theology, they were convinced that believers can and should enjoy the confident hope of salvation. John Calvin correctly taught that such confidence is not some addition to but is actually the essence of faith—since those who truly trust the gospel do so because they inherently enjoy a measure of assurance in it.

When people experience saving faith, they recognize both the truth of the gospel and the wickedness of their sinful condition (cf. Eph. 2:4–6), and they repent of their sins and embrace Jesus Christ as Savior and Lord (Luke 18:13; Acts 2:37–39; cf. 8:35–37;

16:27–34). When that divine work (of conversion and regeneration) takes place (Acts 11:18; 16:14; 18:27), energized by the Holy Spirit, believers sense their new-found faith and are assured of their salvation based on Scripture's promises (e.g., Luke 18:14; John 1:12–13; 3:16; 6:37; 10:9; Acts 13:38–39; Rom. 10:9–13). By setting forth the promises of God upon which salvation rests, the Word of God thus provides believers with an objective source of certainty and, additionally, the Holy Spirit gives subjective assurance through manifest spiritual fruit.

Nearly a century after Calvin, the writers of the Westminster Confession of Faith (1648) composed the following paragraph:

> This infallible assurance doth not so belong to the essence of faith, but that a true believer may wait long, and conflict with many difficulties before he be partaker of it: yet, being enabled by the Spirit to know the things which are freely given him of God, he may, without extraordinary revelation, in the right use of ordinary means, attain thereunto. And therefore it is the duty of everyone to give all diligence to make his calling and election sure, that thereby his heart may be enlarged in peace and joy in the Holy Ghost, in love and thankfulness to God, and in strength and cheerfulness in the duties of obedience, the proper fruits of this assurance; so far is it from inclining men to looseness. (Chapter XVIII, Article III)

Moving beyond some of the earlier Reformers (who had primarily focused on refuting Rome), the Westminster divines addressed the antinomian tendencies of their day by stressing subjective assurance in addition to John Calvin's (and Scripture's) teaching on objective assurance. They emphasized personal examination that would lead believers to recognize practical evidences in their lives of obedience to God's moral law and commands. But some in the church pressed to the extreme the Westminster idea "that a true believer may wait long, and conflict with many difficulties" before gaining full assurance. For example, the seventeenth-century English Puritans' sober, searching preaching caused many people to be so introspective that they often struggled to have assurance. In response, Puritan pastors wrote many treatises to exhort, encourage, and comfort souls that were frightened or insecure, especially expositing what the apostle Paul wrote concerning the Spirit's witness:

> For all who are being led by the Spirit of God, these are sons of God. For you have not received a spirit of slavery leading to fear again, but you have received a spirit of adoption as sons by which we cry out, "Abba! Father!" The Spirit Himself testifies with our spirit that we are children of God. (Rom. 8:14-16)

The witness of this assurance entails the Holy Spirit's working in believers' consciences and emotions so that they feel the joy of their forgiveness and long to be in God's presence, like children with a beloved father. They sense how the Spirit leads and directs them (1 Cor. 2:14-16; Gal. 5:16-18, 25; cf. Luke 24:44-45; Eph. 1:17-19; 3:16-19; Col. 1:9), not through their own wisdom and discernment, but through granting them the desire to live godly lives and obey the Scripture.

To be sure, the Bible clearly teaches that those who are truly saved can never lose their salvation (cf. John 10:35). They have been permanently sealed with the Holy Spirit (Eph. 1:13), and nothing can separate them from the love of their Savior (Rom. 8:38-39). At the same time, however, God's Word also commands every professing Christian to examine his or her life, to see if the salvation that is claimed is actually authentic (2 Cor. 13:5). If salvation is indeed genuine, there will be signs of the Spirit's working in that person's life, both in attitude and behavior. The Bible refers to these attitudes as the "fruit of the Spirit" (Gal. 5:22–23), discussed in the previous chapter. Assurance of salvation, in the subjective sense, comes by examining one's life to see if there is evidence of the Spirit's working in one's attitudes. Such spiritual dispositions manifest themselves in corresponding acts of "love, joy, peace," and so forth, in submission to the commands of Scripture.

John's purpose in writing this epistle is clearly stated in 5:13: "These things I have written to you who believe in the name of the Son of God, so that you may know that you have eternal life." It is to give assurance of salvation to those who might otherwise be led to doubt. So again in our key passage, 2:3–6, John addresses manifest assurance—from the perspective of obedience, which constitutes visible, objective evidence that someone is a Christian. That is a crucial element in John's moral test for believers, an aspect that he divides into three parts: the test stated, the test applied, and the test exemplified.

THE TEST STATED

By this we know that we have come to know Him, if we keep His commandments. (2:3)

"By this" is a transitional phrase John used to introduce a new set of tests that verify salvation and encourage assurance. John presented his readers with some additional ways they could verify that they were walking in the light and had a genuine relationship with God.

The apostle states the case with certainty; he does not say "we hope," "we think," or "we wish," but "we know." "We know" translates the present tense form of the verb *ginōskō*, and means to continually perceive something by experience. Assurance comes from believing and obeying God's commandments in Scripture. Those who fail to do so will and should wonder if they are converted and the Holy Spirit is truly leading them. But obedient believers can be assured that they "have come to know Him [Christ]." The perfect tense of the verb *ginōskō* ("have come to know") looks back on a past action (believing in Jesus Christ for salvation) that has continuing results in the present.

The knowledge of which John spoke is not the mystical "hidden" knowledge of Gnosticism (which promoted a secret, transcendent knowledge whose possessors were members of an elitist religious fraternity), the rationalistic knowledge of Greek philosophy (which taught that unaided human reason could unlock the mysteries of the universe, both natural and supernatural), or the experiential knowledge of hedonism (which claimed that ultimate truth was discovered through experiencing the pleasures of the physical world). Instead, the apostle is pointing to the saving knowledge of Christ that comes from being in a right relationship with Him. John argued that external obedience provides evidence for whether or not an internal reality—that of coming to know Jesus Christ in salvation—has taken place.

Writing to Titus, Paul emphasized the difference between false knowledge and true knowledge: "[Some] profess to know God, but by their deeds they deny Him, being detestable and disobedient and worthless for any good deed" (Titus 1:16; cf. 2 Tim. 3:5, 7).

But that is not true of the Christian faith that John and the other apostles taught. The people who truly know God are those who pursue holy lives, consistent with God's new covenant. The prophet Jeremiah spelled out the nature of that covenant:

> "Behold, days are coming," declares the Lord, "when I will make a new covenant with the house of Israel and with the house of Judah, not like the covenant which I made with their fathers in the day I took them by the hand to bring them out of the land of Egypt, My covenant which they broke, although I was a husband to them," declares the Lord. "But this is the covenant which I will make with the house of Israel after those days," declares the Lord, "I will put My law within them and on their heart I will write it; and I will be their God, and they shall be My people. They will not teach again, each man his neighbor and each man his brother, saying, 'Know the Lord,' for they will all know Me, from the least of them to the greatest of them," declares the Lord, "for I will forgive their iniquity, and their sin I will remember no more." (Jer. 31:31–34)

New-covenant people have God's law written on their hearts, and what is in a person's heart controls how he or she lives. As the writer of Proverbs observed, "For as [a person] thinks in his heart, so is he" (Prov. 23:7, NKJV; cf. 2:10; 3:1; 4:4, 23; Pss. 40:8; 119:10–11; Matt. 6:21; 12:34–35; Rom. 6:17). Israel illustrated well the connection between knowing God and obeying Him. Even though the nation claimed to know Him, she demonstrated the emptiness of that claim by her continual disobedience (Ex. 32:9; Num. 14:11; 25:3; Deut. 9:7, 24; 32:16; Isa. 1:2, 4; 2:8; 29:13; Jer. 2:11–13; 3:6–8; 6:13; 8:5; 31:32; Ezek. 16:59; 33:31; Matt. 15:7–9; Acts 13:27; Rom. 10:3; 2 Cor. 3:13–15). Of course, the obedience that accompanies salvation is not a legalistic obedience, imposed externally or observed superficially and hypocritically; it is a gracious attitude of obedience that flows from the truth embraced internally, following the Holy Spirit's revealing of it through the Word. Even though believers still wrestle with sin (cf. Job 13:23; Ps. 19:13; Rom. 8:13; Heb. 12:1, 4), they can agree with Paul, who wrote,

> I find then the principle that evil is present in me, the one who wants to do good. For I joyfully concur with the law of God in the inner man, but I see a different law in the members of my body, waging war against the law of my mind and making me a prisoner of the law of sin which is in my members. Wretched man that I am! Who will set me free from the body of this death? Thanks be to God through Jesus Christ our Lord! So then, on the one hand I myself with my mind am serving the law of God, but on the other, with my flesh the law of sin. (Rom. 7:21–25)

The word rendered "keep" in 1 John 2:3 (a form of the Greek verb *tēreō*) stresses the idea of an observant, watchful obedience. It can also be translated "guard," which would in this context mean guarding His commandments. Since "keep" is a present, active subjunctive, it conveys the sense of believers' continually safeguarding the commandments because they consider them precious (5:3; Ezra 7:10; Pss. 19:7–8; 119:1, 34, 77, 97, 113, 165; Rom. 7:22). John did not want his readers to settle for a marginal standard of righteousness. Rather the apostle emphasized an obedience that stems from a genuine reverence for God's commands (Ps. 119:66, 172; cf. Acts 17:11; James 1:25).

"Commandments" is from *entolē* ("injunction," "order," or "command"), not *nomos* ("law"). The term refers not to the Mosaic law, but to the precepts and directives of Christ (cf. Matt. 28:19–20). But of course the moral and spiritual precepts the Lord taught were consistent with those revealed to Moses (cf. Matt. 5:17–18; John 5:46), all reflective of God's immutable nature.

Under the new covenant God accepts believers' loving and sincere, albeit imperfect obedience (cf. 1 Kings 8:46; Prov. 20:9) and forgives their disobedience (cf. Pss. 65:3; 103:3; Isa. 43:25). By His grace they display a consistent, heartfelt devotion to the mind of Christ (1 Cor. 2:16; cf. Hos. 6:6) as revealed in the Word (Pss. 1:1–2; 112:1; 119:1–2; Isa. 48:17–18; Luke 11:28). That willing obedience to Scripture in daily living is a reliable indicator both to self and to others that one has come to a saving knowledge of Jesus Christ (cf. Matt. 7:21; John 8:31; 14:21). It differentiates the unregenerate from the regenerate; Paul called the unregenerate "sons of disobedience" (Eph. 2:2), whereas Peter identified the regenerate "as obedient children" (1 Peter 1:14).

God-honoring obedience is really reflective of genuine love; as John wrote later in this epistle, "we love God and observe His commandments. For this is the love of God, that we keep His commandments; and His commandments are not burdensome" (5:2b–3). But this principle was not new to John, as he had heard it from Jesus years earlier in the Upper Room and recorded it in his gospel:

"If you love Me, you will keep My commandments." (John 14:15)

"He who has My commandments and keeps them is the one who loves Me; and he who loves Me will be loved by My Father, and I will love him and will disclose Myself to him." (14:21)

"If anyone loves Me, he will keep My word; and My Father will love him, and We will come to him and make Our abode with him. He who does not love Me does not keep My words; and the word which you hear is not Mine, but the Father's who sent Me." (14:23–24)

"If you keep My commandments, you will abide in My love; just as I have kept My Father's commandments and abide in His love." (15:10)

The Test Applied

The one who says, "I have come to know Him," and does not keep His commandments, is a liar, and the truth is not in him; but whoever keeps His word, in him the love of God has truly been perfected. By this we know that we are in Him: (2:4–5)

In keeping with the nickname Boanerges ("sons of thunder") that Jesus gave him and his brother James, John thunders at those who claim to "have come to know" Christ but do not keep His commandments. As he had earlier done in 1:6 ("If we say that we have fellowship with Him and yet walk in the darkness, we lie and do not practice the truth"), John warns that their claim to fellowship is completely unfounded. Anyone who makes such a claim and lives in disobedience is a liar. The apostle's strong language exposes the danger of self-deception concerning salvation, which is damning to those who fail to realize their blindness, repent of their sins, and embrace the truth (cf. Gal. 6:7; Titus 3:3).

Plainly, those in God's kingdom hear His voice and obey it. Jesus told Pontius Pilate, "Everyone who is of the truth hears My voice" (John 18:37; cf. 1 John 3:18–19). In sharp contrast, those who do not obey His commands demonstrate that "the truth is not in [them]." John therefore exposed the empty pretense of those who assumed they had ascended to a higher level of "divine truth."

For such false teachers, present with the readers, their so-called knowledge elevated them above prosaic earthly matters and rendered unnecessary any concern for moral conduct or godly living. But as James declared, "Even so faith, if it has no works, is dead, being by itself. . . . For just as the body without the spirit is dead, so also faith without works is dead" (James 2:17, 26; cf. Eph. 2:10; Heb. 12:14; 1 Peter 1:14–16). Those whose faith is genuine will obey the truth.

Verse 5 then applies the test for assurance positively. Whoever sincerely and lovingly "keeps His word, in him the love of God has truly been perfected." It is best to understand the phrase translated "the love of God" as an objective genitive, meaning "the love *for* God." John describes the genuine love believers have for God as "perfected," not in the sense of finished perfection, but salvation accomplishment. In fact, this Greek verb *teteleiōtai* is translated "accomplished" in John 4:34; 5:36; and 17:4. The supernatural granting of this love (Rom. 5:5), results in obedience to Scripture, and is not merely an emotional or mystical experience.

It is by this genuine love that believers know that they are in Him. The little phrase "in Him" [Christ] occurs many other places in the New Testament (vv. 8, 27–28; 3:6; 4:13; 5:20; 1 Cor. 1:5; 5:21; Eph. 1:4, 7, 13; 4:21; Phil. 3:9; Col. 2:6–7, 10–11; 2 Thess. 1:12; cf. Col. 1:28) and indicates a central truth of the Christian faith. Commentator John Stott summarized the significance as follows:

> The whole context, and especially verse 6, suggests that the phrase *in Him* again refers to Christ. To be 'in Christ' is Paul's characteristic description of the Christian. But John uses it too. To be (or to 'abide' verse 6) 'in' Him is equivalent to the phrase to 'know' Him (3, 4) and

to 'love' Him (5). Being a Christian consists in essence of a personal relationship to God in Christ, knowing Him, loving Him, and abiding in Him as the branch abides in the vine (Jn. xv. 1 ff.). This is the meaning of 'eternal life' (Jn. xvii. 3; 1 Jn. v. 20).[7]

THE TEST EXEMPLIFIED

the one who says he abides in Him ought himself to walk in the same manner as He walked. (2:6)

The only person who can pass the test of obedience and realize full assurance is the one who . . . abides in Him—because Jesus Christ is the perfect role model for obeying the Father. In John 15:4–5 Jesus commanded,

> "Abide in Me, and I in you. As the branch cannot bear fruit of itself unless it abides in the vine, so neither can you unless you abide in Me. I am the vine, you are the branches; he who abides in Me and I in him, he bears much fruit, for apart from Me you can do nothing." (cf. vv. 10–11)

Believers draw spiritual life from the Lord Jesus Christ, even as branches do from a vine. To abide in Christ is to remain in Him—not a temporary, superficial attachment, but a permanent, deep connection (cf. Luke 9:23; John 6:53–65; Phil. 1:6; 2:11–13). Such authentic abiding in the Savior characterizes those who "continue in the faith firmly established and steadfast, and not moved away from the hope of the gospel that [they] have heard" (Col. 1:23; cf. 2:7; Eph. 3:17), because they are truly regenerate—new creatures who possess irrevocable eternal life.

John made it perfectly clear that those who claim to abide in

Christ must "walk in the same manner as He walked." "Walk" is a metaphor for daily conduct by believers (1:7; John 8:12; 12:35; Rom. 6:4; 8:4; 1 Cor. 7:17; 2 Cor. 5:7; Gal. 5:16; Eph. 2:10; 4:1; 5:2, 8; Col. 1:10; 2:6; 1 Thess. 2:12; 4:1; 2 John 6; cf. Mark 7:5). The Lord Himself perfectly exemplified this principle during His earthly ministry. In every way He obeyed His Father's will:

"For I have come down from heaven, not to do My own will, but the will of Him who sent Me." (John 6:38)

"And He who sent Me is with Me; He has not left Me alone, for I always do the things that are pleasing to Him." (8:29)

"For this reason the Father loves Me, because I lay down My life so that I may take it again. No one has taken it away from Me, but I lay it down on My own initiative. I have authority to lay it down, and I have authority to take it up again. This commandment I received from My Father." (10:17–18)

"So that the world may know that I love the Father, I do exactly as the Father commanded Me." (14:31)

Obviously, believers' obedience will not be perfect, as Jesus' was. Nonetheless, He established the perfect pattern they are to follow. If anyone claims to know Him and abide in Him, it will be evident in his life. He will walk in the light—in the realm of truth and holiness—and guard (obey) Christ's commandments because of his passionate love for the truth and the Lord of the truth. Therein lies the key to real assurance of salvation.

Chapter 6

———⟨✦⟩———

WALKING IN LOVE

Ephesians 5:1–7

Therefore be imitators of God, as beloved children; and walk in love, just as Christ also loved you and gave Himself up for us, an offering and a sacrifice to God as a fragrant aroma. But immorality or any impurity or greed must not even be named among you, as is proper among saints; and there must be no filthiness and silly talk, or coarse jesting, which are not fitting, but rather giving of thanks. For this you know with certainty, that no immoral or impure person or covetous man, who is an idolater, has an inheritance in the kingdom of Christ and God. Let no one deceive you with empty words, for because of these things the wrath of God comes upon the sons of disobedience. Therefore do not be partakers with them; (5:1–7)

In this passage Paul first presents the positive truths about true godly love and then the negative truths about Satan's counterfeit love and its consequences.

The Plea

Therefore be imitators of God, as beloved children; and walk in love, (5:1–2a)

The walk, or conduct, of the believer is a key matter to Paul. He has introduced the fact that ours is to be a worthy walk (4:1) and a walk different from that of unbelievers (4:17). He will also call for a walk in light (5:8) and a walk in wisdom (5:15). In this verse the apostle pleads with believers to walk in such a way that daily life is characterized by love. Growing in love is a continuing need for every believer, since love fulfills all of God's law (Rom. 13:8–10). As we grow in love we also see the need to be even more loving. And since biblically defined love is so contrary to the flesh, we are always in need of reminders and encouragement to love.

Imitating the Source

"Therefore" refers back to the last part of chapter 4, especially verse 32. Kindness, tenderheartedness, and forgiveness are characteristics of God, who *is* love. God Himself is infinitely kind, tenderhearted, and forgiving, and we achieve those virtues by imitating their Source.

Mimētēs ("imitators") is the term from which we get *mimic,* someone who copies specific characteristics of another person. As "imitators of God," Christians are to imitate God's characteristics, and above all His love. The whole of the Christian life is the reproduction of godliness as seen in the person of Christ. God's purpose in salvation is to redeem men from sin and to conform them "to the image of His Son" (Rom. 8:29). To be conformed to Christ is to become perfect, just as God is perfect (Matt. 5:48). "As obedient children," Peter tells us, "do not be conformed to the former lusts which were yours in your ignorance, but like the Holy One who called you, be holy yourselves also in all your behavior; because it is written, 'You shall be holy, for I am holy' " (1 Peter 1:14–16; cf. Lev. 11:44). The great hope of believers is, "We know that when

He appears, we will be like Him, because we will see Him just as He is" (1 John 3:2). Imitating His love is possible because "the love of God has been poured out within our hearts through the Holy Spirit who was given to us" (Rom.5:5).

When Alexander the Great discovered a coward in his army who also was named Alexander, he told the soldier, "Renounce your cowardice or renounce your name." Those who carry God's name are to be imitators of His character. By His grace it is possible to reflect Him even in our present limitations.

To know what God is like we must study His Word, His revelation of Himself, His great self-disclosure. Yet the more we learn of God's character the more we learn how far above us He is and how impossible in ourselves it is to fulfill the command to be like Him, to be absolutely perfect, just as He is. That is why we need "to be strengthened with power through His Spirit in the inner man" in order to "be filled up to all the fullness of God" (Eph. 3:16, 19). The only way we can become imitators of God is for the Lord Jesus Christ to live His perfect life through us. We are totally dependent on His Spirit to become like Him. If we are to obey Paul's admonition to the Corinthians, "let all that you do be done in love" (1 Cor. 16:14), we must submit to the controlling influence of the Spirit.

It is natural for children to be like their parents. They have their parents' nature and they instinctively imitate their parents' actions and behavior. Through Jesus Christ God has given us the right to become His children (John 1:12; Gal. 3:26). As Paul declared at the beginning of this letter, God "predestined us to adoption as sons through Jesus Christ to Himself, according to the kind intention of His will" (Eph. 1:5). Because our heavenly Father is holy, we are to be holy. Because He is kind, we are to be kind. Because He is forgiving, we are to be forgiving. Because God in Christ humbled

Himself, we are to humble ourselves. Because God is love, as His "beloved children" we are to walk in love. This ability is not natural, however, but supernatural—requiring a new nature and the continuous power of the Holy Spirit flowing through us by obedience to God's Word.

The Greatest Proof of Love: Undeserved Forgiveness

The greatest evidence of love is undeserved forgiveness. The supreme act of God's love was to give "His only begotten Son, that whoever believes in Him shall not perish, but have eternal life" (John 3:16). God's love brought man's forgiveness. God loved the world with such a great love that He offered forgiveness to sinful, rebellious, wretched, vile mankind, by sending His own Son to give His life on the cross that they might not suffer death. He offered the world the free gift of eternal fellowship with Him.

Because forgiveness is the supreme evidence of God's love, it will also be the most convincing proof of our love. Love will always lead us to forgive others just as love led God in Christ to forgive us (Eph. 4:32). Nothing more clearly discloses a hard, loveless heart than lack of forgiveness. Lack of forgiveness betrays a lack of love. The presence of forgiveness always proves the presence of love, because only love has the motive and power to forgive. The extent of our love is the extent of our ability to forgive.

Whatever another believer may do against us, no matter how terrible or destructive or unjustified, Christ has paid the penalty for that sin. No matter how others may hurt, slander, persecute, or in any way harm us, Christ's sacrifice was sufficient to pay their penalty. When a Christian expresses, or even harbors, vengeance toward a brother, he not only sins by allowing selfish hatred to control him but he sins by profaning Christ's sacrifice—by seeking to mete out punishment for a sin whose penalty has already been paid by his Lord.

Because Christ has paid the penalty for every sin, we have no right to hold any sin against any person, even a nonbeliever. Peter thought that forgiving someone "up to seven times" was generous. But Jesus said, "I do not say to you, up to seven times, but up to seventy times seven" (Matt. 18:22). In Christ *all* our "sins have been forgiven . . . for His name's sake" (1 John 2:12); He has "forgiven us *all* our transgressions" (Col. 2:13, emphasis added). "In Him we have redemption through His blood, the forgiveness of our trespasses, according to the riches of His grace" (Eph. 1:7).

Just as the depth of God's love is shown by how much He has forgiven, the depth of our love is shown by how much we forgive. "Above all," Peter says, "keep fervent in your love for one another, because love covers a multitude of sins" (1 Peter 4:8). The Greek word behind "fervent" refers to a muscle stretched to the limit. Our love is to stretch to the limit in order to cover "a multitude of sins." The greater our love, the greater the multitude of sins it will cover in forgiveness.

The depth of our love is also shown by how much we know we have been forgiven. When Jesus was eating dinner with Simon the Pharisee, a prostitute came into the house and anointed Jesus' feet with her tears and with expensive perfume. Simon was incensed at what she did and was disappointed in Jesus for allowing such a woman to touch Him. Jesus responded by telling a parable: "'A moneylender had two debtors: one owed five hundred denarii, and the other fifty. When they were unable to repay, he graciously forgave them both. So which of them will love him more?' Simon answered and said, 'I suppose the one whom he forgave more.' And He said to him, 'You have judged correctly.'" After comparing the ways that Simon and the woman had treated Him, Jesus said, "For this reason I say to you, her sins, which are many, have been forgiven, for she loved much; but he who is forgiven little, loves little" (Luke 7:36–47).

Because Simon had no real sense of the enormity of the sin in his own life, and therefore sensed no need for forgiveness, he was unforgiving of others—especially those whom he considered moral and social outcasts. Unforgivingness is the measure of self-righteousness just as forgiveness is the measure of love. Our ability to love, and therefore to forgive, depends on our sense of how much God has forgiven us. Unforgivingness is also a measure of unbelief, because the person who feels no need for forgiveness feels no need for God.

In George MacDonald's novel *Robert Falconer*, the protagonist was sharing his faith with destitute people in a certain city and read them the story of the woman who wiped Jesus' feet with her tears. During his reading, Falconer heard a loud sob and looked up at a young girl whose face was disfigured by smallpox.

"Will he ever come again?" she sobbed.

"Who?" asked Falconer.

"Him—Jesus Christ. I've heard tell, I think, that he was to come again some day."

"Why do you ask?"

"Because—" she said, with a fresh burst of tears, which rendered the words that followed unintelligible. But she recovered herself in a few moments, and, as if finishing her sentence, put her hand up to her poor, thin, colourless hair, and said, "My hair ain't long enough to wipe his feet."

"Do you know what he would say to you, my girl?" Falconer asked.

"No. What would he say to me?..."

"He would say: Thy sins are forgiven thee."[1]

The person who recognizes the greatness of his own forgiveness by God's love will himself in love be forgiving. He forgives in love because his heavenly Father has forgiven in love and he desires to be an imitator of his Father.

The Pattern

just as Christ also loved you and gave Himself up for us, an offering and a sacrifice to God as a fragrant aroma. (5:2b)

A young child often learns to draw by tracing. The more carefully she traces, the truer the likeness of her copy is to the original.

The pattern for Christian living is Christ Himself, the one by whom all believers are to trace their lives. The great difference between this tracing and that of the young child learning to draw is that we will never have a time when Christ will cease to be our pattern. And we will never be "on our own," sufficiently skilled in ourselves to live as He lived. In fact, our part is not so much to pattern our lives ourselves as to allow God's Spirit to pattern us after His Son. Second Corinthians 3:18 expresses this profound truth in magnificent terms: "But we all, with unveiled face, beholding as in a mirror the glory of the Lord, are being transformed into the same image from glory to glory, just as from the Lord, the Spirit."

Unconditional Love

The *summum bonum* of Christ that we are to imitate is His love. He "loved [us] and gave Himself up for us." Giving of oneself to others is the epitome of *agapē* love. Biblical love is not a pleasant emotion or good feeling about someone, but the giving of oneself for another's welfare (cf. 1 John 3:16). Divine love is unconditional love, love that depends entirely on the one who loves and not on the merit, attractiveness, or response of the one loved. Christ did not simply have a deep feeling and emotional concern for mankind. Nor did He sacrifice Himself for us because we were deserving (cf. Rom. 5:8, 10). "While we were yet sinners," He "gave Himself up for us" purely out of sovereign, gracious love, taking our sin upon Himself and paying its penalty in our behalf.

God's love, and all love that is like His, moves into action for the sake of giving, not getting. With conditional love, if the conditions are not met there is no obligation to love. If we do not get, we do not give. But God makes no conditions for His love to us and commands that we love others without conditions. There is no way to earn God's love or to deserve it by reason of human goodness.

Romantic, emotional love between husband and wife ebbs and flows, and sometimes disappears altogether. But loss of romantic love is never an appropriate excuse for dissolving a marriage, because the love that God specifically commands husbands to have for their wives is *agapē* love (Eph. 5:25; 3:19; cf. Titus 2:4; etc.)—love like His own undeserved love for us, love that is based on willful choice in behalf of the one loved, regardless of emotions or attraction. Romantic love enhances and beautifies the relationship between husband and wife, but the binding force of a Christian marriage is God's own kind of love, the love that loves because it is the divine nature to love. It is the love of giving, not of getting; and even when it ceases to get, it continues to give. Where there is the sacrificial love of willful choice, there is also likely to be the love of intimacy, feeling, and friendship (Greek *philia*).

God loved us while we were still sinners and enemies, and He continues to love us as believers, even though we continue to sin and fall short of His perfection and His glory. He loves us when we forget Him, when we disobey Him, when we deny Him, when we fail to return His love, and when we grieve His Holy Spirit. When Jude said, "Keep yourselves in the love of God" (Jude 21), he was indicating the responsibility to stay in the place where that divine love sheds its blessing.

Those who are given God's nature through Jesus Christ are commanded to love as God loves. In Christ, it is now *our* nature to love just as it is God's nature to love—because His nature is now our nature. For a Christian not to love is for him to live against his or her own nature, as well as against God's.

Lovelessness is therefore more than a failure or shortcoming. It is sin, a willful disobedience of God's command and disregard of His example. To love as God loves is to love *because* God loves, because we are to "be imitators of God, as beloved children" and because "Christ also loved [us], and gave Himself up for us, an offering and a sacrifice to God."

Self-Sacrificing Love

God's love not only is forgiving and unconditional but is also self-sacrificing. Therefore to love as God loves is to love sacrificially, to love by the giving of ourselves as He gave Himself.

The Christian's walk in love is to extend to every person—believer and unbeliever. If God's love can reach out even to His enemies, how can we refuse to love our enemies? If He loves His imperfect children with a perfect love, how can we not love fellow believers, whose imperfections we share? And if divine love led Christ to sacrifice Himself for unworthy and ungrateful sinners, how can we not give ourselves to fellow sinful people, unbelievers as well as believers, in His name?

Shortly before His betrayal and arrest, Jesus was having supper with His disciples. During the meal the disciples began arguing among themselves as to which was the greatest. Their Lord was facing His ultimate humiliation and affliction, and yet their only concern was for themselves, for their own prestige, rank, and glory. When the Lord most needed their comfort, encouragement, and support, they acted as if He were not with them. All their attention was focused selfishly on themselves (Luke 22:24).

It was then that Jesus picked up a basin of water and began washing their feet, a task usually reserved for the lowest of servants. Despite their callous lack of concern for His impending suffering and death, Jesus humbly, forgivingly, unconditionally, and self-sacrificially ministered to them. The apostle John records Jesus' words after the Master had finished washing their feet and returned to the supper table:

> He said to them, "Do you know what I have done to you? You call Me Teacher and Lord; and you are right, for so I am. If I then, the Lord and the Teacher, washed your feet, you also ought to wash one another's feet. For I gave you an example that you also should do as I did to you. Truly, truly, I say to you, a slave is not greater than his master, nor is one who is sent greater than the one who sent him." (John 13:12–16)

Later Jesus would command His disciples to love in this same manner (vv. 34–35).

In giving "Himself up for us, an offering and a sacrifice to God," Christ became a fragrant aroma to His heavenly Father, a sacrifice that demonstrated in the fullest and most ultimate way God's kind of love. The words for us indicate the personal expression of love directed at all who believe. (This does not limit the provision of the atonement only to believers, as other Scriptures make clear. See John 1:29; 3:15–16; Rom. 10:13; 2 Cor. 5:14; 1 Tim. 2:4, 6; 4:10; 2 Pet. 2:1; 1 John 2:2; 4:14.)

The first five chapters of Leviticus describe five offerings commanded by God of the Israelites. The first three were the burnt offering, the meal offering, and the peace offering. The burnt offering (Lev. 1:1–17) depicted Christ's total devotion to God in giving His very life to obey and please His Father; the meal (grain) offering (Lev. 2:1–16) depicted Christ's perfection, and the peace offering (Lev. 3:1–17; 4:27–31) depicted His making peace between God and man. All of those offerings obviously spoke of what was pleasing to God. Of each, the Scripture says it provided a "soothing aroma to the Lord" (Lev. 1:9, 13, 17; 2:2, 9, 12; 3:5, 16). Philippians 4:18 explains that the fragrant aroma meant the sacrifice was "acceptable . . . well-pleasing to God." But the other two offerings—the sin (Lev. 4:1–26, 32–35) and the trespass (Lev. 5:1–19) offerings—were repulsive to God, because, though they depicted Christ, they depicted Him as bearing the sin of mankind. They depicted the Father's turning His back on the Son when "He made Him who knew no sin to be sin on our behalf" (2 Cor. 5:21), at which time Jesus exclaimed from the cross, "My God, My God, why have You forsaken Me?" (Matt. 27:46).

While Christ was the sin-bearer, God could not look on Him. But when the Father raised Christ from the dead, the sacrifice that caused Him to become the sin-bearer became the sacrifice that conquered sin. The sin that put Him to death was itself put to death, and that great act of love was to God as a fragrant aroma. That aroma spreads its fragrance to everyone on earth who will place themselves under the grace of that sacrifice, and it will spread its fragrance throughout heaven for all eternity. In all aspects, our lives should please God (cf. 2 Cor. 2:14–16).

THE PERVERSION

But immorality or any impurity or greed must not even be named among you, as is proper among saints; and there must be no filthiness and silly talk, or coarse jesting, which are not fitting, but rather giving of thanks. (5:3–4)

Counterfeit Love

Whatever God establishes, Satan will counterfeit. Where God establishes true love, Satan produces counterfeit love. Counterfeit love characterizes Satan's children, those who are of the world, just as true love characterizes God's children, those who are citizens of heaven.

In contrast to godly, unselfish, forgiving love, the world's love is lustful and self-indulgent. It loves because the object of love is attractive, enjoyable, pleasant, satisfying, appreciative, loves in return, produces desired feelings, or is likely to repay in some way. It is always based on the other person's fulfilling one's own needs and desires and meeting one's own expectations.

In summary, worldly love is reciprocal, giving little in the expectation of getting much. Speaking of that kind of love, Jesus said, "For if you love those who love you, what reward do you have? Do not even the tax collectors do the same?" (Matt. 5:46).

The world claims to want love, and love is advocated and praised from every corner. Romantic love especially is touted. Songs, novels, movies, and television serials continually exploit emotional, lustful desire as if it were genuine love. Questing for and fantasizing about the "perfect love" is portrayed as the ultimate human experience.

The Result: Immorality and Impurity

It should not be surprising that the misguided quest for that kind of love leads inevitably to immorality and impurity, because that kind of love is selfish and destructive, a deceptive counterfeit of God's love. It is always conditional and is always self-centered. It is not concerned about commitment but only satisfaction; it is not concerned about giving but only getting. It has no basis for permanence because its purpose is to use and to exploit rather than to serve and to help. It lasts until the one loved no longer satisfies or until he or she disappears for someone else.

The Greek word for "immorality" in verse 3, *porneia*, refers to all sexual sin, and all sexual sin is against God and against godly love. It is the antonym of *enkrateia*, which refers to self-control, especially in the area of sex. When Paul spoke before the Roman governor Felix and his wife, Drusilla, "discussing righteousness, self-control and the judgment to come, Felix became frightened and said, 'Go away for the present, and when I find time I will summon you'" (Acts 24:24–25). Felix had stolen Drusilla from her former husband and was therefore living with her in an adulterous relationship. The sexual self-control of which Paul spoke pertained to lustful passion, as Felix understood. The message to the governor was that he was living contrary to God's righteousness by refusing to discipline his sexual desire, and for that he was subject to God's judgment.

Loss of sexual self-control leads to its opposite, which is immorality and impurity. *Akatharsia* ("impurity") is a more general term than *porneia*, referring to anything that is unclean and filthy.

Jesus used the word to describe the rottenness of decaying bodies in a tomb (Matt. 23:27). The other ten times the word is used in the New Testament it is associated with sexual sin. It refers to immoral thoughts, passions, ideas, fantasies, and every other form of sexual corruption.

Contemporary society's obsession with sex has even found its way into the church. The influence of the lustful world has been so pervasive and the church so weak and undiscerning that many Christians have become convinced that all sorts of sexual excesses and impurities are covered by grace or can be rendered morally safe if engaged in with the right attitude—especially if some Scripture verse can be twisted to give seeming support. But immorality and impurity cannot be sanctified or modified into anything better than what they are, which is wickedness—a crime against the holy God and the loving Savior. In 1 Corinthians 5:1–5 and 6:13–20 Paul shows that there is no place for that in the Christian life.

Greed is inseparable from impurity. Every form of sexual immorality is an expression of the self-will, self-gratification, and self-centeredness of greed. It is by nature contrary to love, which is self-giving. Immorality and impurity are but forms of greed in the realm of sexual sin. They are manifestations of sexual covetousness and express counterfeit love (which is really hate, since love seeks the purity of others and is unselfish), masquerading as something beautiful, good, and rewarding. Because those sins seem so attractive and promising, spouses are forsaken, children are neglected, homes are destroyed, friends are disregarded, as no effort is spared to fulfill the desire of a lustful fantasy—all in the name of love.

Because of the strong sexual nature of human beings, sexual sins are powerful and can become perverted in unimaginable ways. If given free rein, sexual sins lead to complete insensitivity to the feelings and welfare of others, to horrible brutality, and even to murder—as news stories testify daily.

That is why the sins of "immorality or any impurity or greed [should] not even be named among [Christians], as is proper among saints." Those sins cannot in any way be justified, and they should not in any way be tolerated. The meaning of "saints" is "holy ones," and those who are holy have nothing to do with that which is unholy.

Related Sins: Filthiness, Silly Talk, and Coarse Jesting

Paul continues his warning against this perversion of love by mentioning an extensive list of related sins that is sure to cover every believer at one time or another. Not only should Christians never engage in sexual sins of any kind, but they should never be guilty of "filthiness and silly talk, or coarse jesting."

"Filthiness" has to do with general obscenity, any talk that is degrading and disgraceful. It comes from the same Greek root as "disgraceful" in verse 12, where Paul says that such vile things should not even be mentioned, much less participated in, and is related to the term in Colossians 3:8, meaning "dirty speech."

"Silly talk," from the Greek word *mōrologia* and used only here in the New Testament, is derived from *mōros* (which means dull or stupid, and is the word from which we get moron) and *legō* (to speak). It is stupid talk, talk only befitting someone who is intellectually deficient. It is sometimes referred to as low obscenity, foolish talk that comes from the drunk or the gutter mouth. It has no point except to give an air of dirty worldliness.

"Coarse jesting" on the other hand, refers to talk that is more pointed and determined, from the Greek word *eutrapelia*. It carries the idea of quickly turning something that is said or done—no matter how innocent—into that which is obscene or suggestive. It is the filthy talk of a person who uses every word and circumstance to display his immoral wit. It is the stock-in-trade of the clever talk-show host who is never at a loss for sexual innuendo. But the low obscenity of silly talk and the "high" obscenity of coarse jesting come from the same kind of heart, the heart given over to moral filthiness.

In light of such clear teaching of God's Word, it is strange that so many Christians not only discuss but laugh and joke with impunity about almost every form of sexual intimacy, corruption, and perversion. But God's standard is clear: "There must be no filthiness and silly talk, or coarse jesting, which are not fitting."

The Proper Replacement

Instead of being involved in immorality or filthy speaking, the believer's mouth should be involved in the giving of thanks. Thanksgiving is an expression of unselfishness. The selfish and unloving person does not give thanks because he thinks he deserves whatever good thing he receives. The unselfish and loving person, on the other hand, focuses his life and his concern on the needs of others. Whatever good thing he receives from God or from other people he counts as undeserved and gracious. He is always thankful because his spirit is one of loving and of giving. Instead of using others, he serves them. Instead of trying to turn the innocent into the immoral, he seeks to change the immoral into what is righteous and holy. He is thankful because the holy life is the satisfying life, and people see love for God in the thankful person.

If Christians are known for anything it should be for love expressed toward God and others by unceasing thankfulness (cf.

1 Thess. 5:18, where the injunction is clear: "In everything give thanks; for this is God's will for you in Christ Jesus.")

THE PUNISHMENT

For this you know with certainty, that no immoral or impure person or covetous man, who is an idolater, has an inheritance in the kingdom of Christ and God. Let no one deceive you with empty words, for because of these things the wrath of God comes upon the sons of disobedience. Therefore do not be partakers with them; (5:5–7)

It is clear that Paul is restating a truth he had taught the Ephesians many times while he pastored among them and, no doubt, one that others had reinforced. "For this you know with certainty," he said. There should have been no confusion or doubt in their minds about what he was about to say, because it was nothing new.

God does not tolerate sin, and perverted love leads to punishment. Sin has no place in His kingdom and no place in His family. "Immoral," "impure," and "covetous" are from the same basic Greek words as "immorality," "impurity," and "greed" in verse 3. Covetousness is a form of idolatry. The covetous man, therefore, is more than simply selfish and immoral; he is an idolater (cf. Col. 3:5).

Persons who are characterized by the sins Paul has just condemned in verses 3 and 4 will have no inheritance in the kingdom of Christ and God. No person whose life pattern is one of habitual immorality, impurity, and greed can be a part of God's kingdom, because no such person belongs to Him. Such actions and attitudes would contradict the truths of Romans 6 and 2 Corinthians 5:17, as well as the instruction of First John regarding the characteristics of believers. The life described here testifies to an unredeemed, sinful nature—no matter what relationship to Christ a person might claim to have. God's children have God's nature, and the habitually sinful person proves that he does not have a godly nature (1 John 3:9–10). "The kingdom of Christ and God" refers to the sphere of salvation, the community of the redeemed, and the place of eternal glory. The kingdom is the rule of Christ and God, which includes the present church, the future millennium, and the eternal state in glory.

"For the grace of God has appeared, bringing salvation to all men, instructing us to deny ungodliness and worldly desires and to live sensibly, righteously and godly in the present age" (Titus 2:11–12). Every person who is saved, and is therefore a part of that glorious rule of Christ and God, is instructed by the Holy Spirit and by the inclination of his new nature to forsake sin and to seek righteousness. The person whose basic life pattern does not reflect that orientation cannot claim God as his Father or the kingdom of Christ and God as his inheritance.

It is dangerously deceptive for Christians to try to give assurance of salvation to someone who has no biblical grounds for such assurance. In his first letter to the church at Corinth, Paul gives an even more detailed listing of sins whose habitual practice proves a person is not saved and has no claim on God. "Do you not know that the unrighteous will not inherit the kingdom of God? Do not be deceived; neither fornicators, nor idolaters, nor adulterers, nor effeminate, nor homosexuals, nor thieves, nor the covetous, nor drunkards, nor revilers, nor swindlers, will inherit the kingdom of God" (1 Cor. 6:9–10). Such things do not characterize the children of God (cf. Gal. 5:17–21 for a similar insight). The verdict of God is that, no matter what may be the claim, a life dominated by sin like this is damned to hell.

People will try to deny that, but Paul warns not to listen to them. "Let no one deceive you with empty words," telling you that sin is tolerable and that God will not exclude unrepentant sinners from His kingdom. Empty words are full of error, devoid of truth, and therefore they deceive.

It is because of these things, that is, because of the sins listed here and the lies of empty words, that "the wrath of God comes upon the sons of disobedience." Such people are called sons of disobedience (see also 2:2) because it is their nature to disobey and they are "children of wrath" (2:3; cf. 2 Thess. 1:8–10), the targets for God's guns of judgment.

God's attitude toward perverted love and sexual sin is seen clearly in Numbers 25:1–9, where the Israelites had relations with Moabite women and God slaughtered 24,000 of them. His attitude toward sexual sin has not changed, and perverted love attracts God's wrath like a fully lit city attracts enemy bombers.

In a final warning, Paul writes, "Therefore do not be partakers with them." In effect, he says, "Don't join the world in its evil." Don't be partners with them in wickedness. Be partners with Christ in righteousness. Don't imitate the world, but rather "be imitators of God, as beloved children" (v. 1).

———— ⚬∞⚬ ————

Chapter 7

WALKING IN WISDOM

EPHESIANS 5:15–17

Therefore be careful how you walk, not as unwise men, but as wise, making the most of your time, because the days are evil. So then do not be foolish, but understand what the will of the Lord is. (5:15–17)

The word *fool* commonly refers to a person who acts unintelligently and irresponsibly. But Scripture defines a fool as a person who says "in his heart, 'There is no God'" and who is morally corrupt, doing "abominable deeds" (Ps. 14:1). The fool is the person who lives apart from God—either as a theological or practical atheist or as both, denying God by his actions as well as his words. The supreme fool is the person who has anti-God thinking and living patterns.

Because men are born separated from God and with hearts that are naturally against Him (Rom. 5:8, 10; Eph. 2:3; Col. 1:21) they are born spiritually foolish. "For even though they knew God, they did not honor Him as God or give thanks; but they became futile in their speculations, and their foolish heart was darkened. Professing to be wise, they became fools" (Rom. 1:21–22). "A natural man does not accept the things of the Spirit of God, for they are foolishness to him; and he cannot understand them, because they are spiritually appraised" (1 Cor. 2:14). The natural man has the most important things in life exactly reversed. Consequently, he thinks foolishness is wisdom and wisdom is foolishness.

THE SPIRITUAL FOOL AND TRUE WISDOM

No man can live without a god of some sort, and the spiritual fool inevitably substitutes a false god for the true God. He creates gods of his own making (Rom. 1:21–23) and, in effect, becomes his own god, his own authority in all things. "The way of a fool is right in his own eyes" (Prov. 12:15), and therefore he determines right and wrong and truth and falsehood entirely by his own fallen thinking and sinful inclination.

When the fool sets himself up as his own god, he will naturally "mock at sin" (Prov. 14:9). Sin is that which is against God, and since the fool does not recognize God, he does not recognize sin. The spiritually self-sufficient fool makes his own rules and justifies his own behavior, and in doing so he refuses to acknowledge sin and its consequences.

The fool cannot help spreading his foolishness. The more he is convinced of the wisdom of his folly, the more he will seek to propagate it. By what he says and by what he does he gives continual testimony to his denial of God, to his becoming his own god, and to his mocking of sin. No matter what his intellectual level, academic achievements, talents, wealth, or reputation, the mouth of the natural man can spiritually do nothing but spout folly (Prov. 15:2).

The unregenerate person is a fool because he denies God by belief and by practice. He is a fool because he becomes his own god. He is a fool because he mocks sin. And he is a fool because he contaminates the rest of society with the ungodly foolishness that damns his own soul. He bequeaths his legacy of foolishness to his children, his friends, and his society—to everyone who falls under the influence of his folly.

"Because they hated knowledge, and did not choose the fear of the Lord," the writer of Proverbs says of fools, "they shall eat of the fruit of their own way and be satiated with their own devices. For the waywardness of the naive will kill them, and the complacency of fools will destroy them" (Prov. 1:29, 31–32).

The Growth of Knowledge

The knowledge that the ungodly person hates is not practical knowledge. On the contrary, he prides himself on factual knowledge. Someone has estimated that, if all of man's accumulated knowledge from the beginning of recorded history to 1845 were represented by one inch, what he learned from 1845 until 1945 would amount to three inches and what he learned from 1945 until 1975 would represent the height of the Washington Monument! Inventor, innovator, and mathematician Buckminster Fuller presented his Knowledge Doubling Curve in his 1982 bestseller *Critical Path*, arguing that our acquisition of knowledge at the end of World War II had jumped from doubling approximately each century to doubling every twenty-five years, and would continue to accelerate, its rate approaching a steep "J curve" in rapid ascent.[1] By the 2010s "nanotechnology [has been] doubling every two years and clinical knowledge every eighteen months. But on average human knowledge is doubling every 13 months," wrote researcher David Russell Schilling.[2] And IBM has forecast that "the build out of the 'internet of things' will lead to the doubling of knowledge every 12 hours."[3]

Few people, however, would argue that the incredible leap in scientific, technological, and other such knowledge has been paralleled by a corresponding leap in common-sense wisdom, not to mention spiritual and moral wisdom. If anything, man's understanding of what he is doing and why he is doing it seems to decrease as his practical knowledge increases. The more learned he becomes in that superficial kind of knowledge, the less need he sees for the knowledge that comes only from God.

Therefore the ultimate destiny of fools is that they are "always learning and never able to come to the knowledge of the truth" (2 Tim. 3:7) and they "die for lack of understanding" (Prov. 10:21) even while accumulating great amounts of information. They become smarter and more foolish at the same time. Foolishness comes from trusting in purely human knowledge and excluding divine knowledge. Men's foolishness increases with their knowledge only when their self-reliance increases. The natural, unregenerate man suffers from his congenital and terminal foolishness because he will not submit to God. He accumulates vast knowledge apart from God, but spiritual understanding and divine wisdom elude him. He hates the truth about sin and salvation.

Where Wisdom Begins

Wisdom begins with fear of the Lord (Prov. 1:7) and continues by acknowledging His truth and ways. "Righteous men, wise men, and their deeds are in the hand of God" (Eccles. 9:1). The way to wisdom and the way to life is the way of God. The only power that can overcome a man's foolishness and turn him to wisdom is salvation, turning to God through Jesus Christ. Turning from foolishness to wisdom is turning from self to God. And it is God's own Word that is "able to give [us] the wisdom that leads to salvation through faith which is in Christ Jesus" (2 Tim. 3:15).

The kind of wisdom the Bible praises is not that prized by the ancient Greeks who were Paul's contemporaries. Their wisdom was characterized by philosophy and sophistry, the endless spinning and discussion of theories that have no real relation to life, that have no bearing on God or on practical living. The Greeks could, and often did, go from philosophy to philosophy without changing their basic attitudes or their basic way of life. They were simply playing the game of philosophy, with the sort of wisdom that does not *want* to come to the knowledge of the truth, because—unlike hypotheses and speculations—truth demands recognition, acceptance, and change.

In Scripture, on the other hand, wisdom is centered in conviction and behavior, specifically in recognizing and obeying God. When a person comes to Christ, he leaves the realm of foolishness and enters the realm of wisdom. Just as being a Christian leads him to walk worthily (4:1), humbly (4:2), in unity (4:3–16), separated from the world's ways (4:17–32), in love (5:1–7), and in light (5:8–14), it also leads him to walk in wisdom (5:15–17).

In the present passage, Paul mentions three things that the Lord's wisdom teaches His child. The wise believer knows his life principles, his limited privileges, and his Lord's purposes.

THE BELIEVER'S LIFE PRINCIPLES

Therefore be careful how you walk, not as unwise men, but as wise, (5:15)

The literal meaning of the Greek term translated "be" in verse 15 is "look or observe," and Paul's command for believers to see that they walk carefully is based on what he has just been teaching.

"Therefore" refers immediately back to the apostle's call for believers to walk as those who have been raised from the dead and are living in Christ's light (v. 14). It also reaches even further back to build upon his call for believers to be imitators of their heavenly Father (5:1). Christians are to walk wisely rather than unwisely because they are God's beloved children, saved through the sacrifice of His beloved Son (5:1–2). Only the wise walk befits the children of God.

Act Like Who You Are

Just as they are to walk in humility, unity, separation, love, and light (4:1–5:14), Christians are also to walk in wisdom. In other words, they are to live like the people they *are*. In Christ we *are* one, we *are* separated, we *are* love, we *are* light, and we *are* wise—and what we do should correspond to what we are.

At salvation every believer has been made wise. Paul wrote to Timothy: "You have known the sacred writings which are able to give you the wisdom that leads to salvation through faith which is in Christ Jesus" (2 Tim. 3:15). By God's grace, the saved "are in Christ Jesus, who became to us wisdom from God, and righteousness and sanctification, and redemption" (1 Cor. 1:30). Just as in Christ God miraculously makes us immediately righteous, sanctified, and redeemed, He also makes us immediately wise. The moment we were saved we became a repository of wisdom that henceforth renders us responsible for our behavior. Because we are in Christ, "the treasures of wisdom and knowledge" that are hidden in Him (Col. 2:3) are therefore also hidden in us.

John wrote of the Holy Spirit, the resident truth teacher in the life of every saint: "But you have an anointing from the Holy One, and you all know. I have not written to you because you do not know the truth, but because you do know it" (1 John 2:20–21).

Further, he said, "You have no need for anyone [any human teacher with simply human wisdom] to teach you," because "His anointing teaches you about all things, and is true" (v. 27). We cannot have salvation without God's wisdom any more than we can have salvation without his righteousness, sanctification, and redemption.

How different from the "easy believism" of the contemporary church, which purports to offer salvation in segments. First it is claimed that men are born again by accepting Christ as Savior. Then, as they grow in grace, they may renounce sin; start pursuing righteousness, sanctification, and wisdom; and receive Him as Lord. But Paul said, "For the grace of God has appeared, bringing salvation to all men, instructing us to deny ungodliness and worldly desires and to live sensibly, righteously and godly in the present age" (Titus 2:11–12). The very first instruction of the gospel to the saved person is to renounce and forsake sin and to live a godly, righteous life. That instruction, or wisdom, is a part of the new birth, not something subsequent to it.

As Jesus made clear in the Beatitudes, among the first and most necessary marks of salvation are mourning over sin and hungering and thirsting for righteousness (Matt. 5:4, 6). As Paul made clear in the beginning of this letter, "In all wisdom and insight [God] made known to us the mystery of His will" (Eph. 1:8–9).

It is not that we do not grow in wisdom as we mature in the Christian life. We are specifically commanded to "grow in the grace and knowledge of our Lord and Savior Jesus Christ" (2 Pet. 3:18). As we become more and more conformed to our Lord and Savior, we will grow more and more in His love, joy, peace, and in every other fruit of the Spirit (Gal. 5:22–23). In another of God's divine paradoxes, we grow in what we have already been given in fullness. We grow practically in what we already possess positionally. Even

Jesus "kept increasing in wisdom" (Luke 2:52), and some believers in the Jerusalem church were "full of . . . wisdom" (Acts 6:3).

Speaking to believers, James said, "If any of you lacks wisdom, let him ask of God, who gives to all generously and without reproach, and it will be given to him" (James 1:5). Paul prayed that the Colossian believers would "be filled with the knowledge of His will in all spiritual wisdom and understanding" and that they would "let the word of Christ richly dwell within [them], with all wisdom teaching and admonishing one another" (Col. 1:9; 3:16). The believer begins his new life in Christ with all the wisdom necessary to live for His Lord, but he is also to continually grow in wisdom, that he can be even more mature, more faithful, and more productive in His service.

Walk with Care . . .

Akribōs ("careful") has the basic meaning of accurate and exact, and carries the associated idea of looking, examining, and investigating something with great care. It also carries the idea of alertness. As believers walk through the spiritual mine field of the world, they are to be constantly alert to every danger that Satan puts in their way. That is why Jesus warned that "the gate is small and the way is narrow that leads to life" (Matt. 7:14).

If it had not been written centuries before the time of Paul, Proverbs 2 would appear to be a commentary on Ephesians 5:15. Throughout the chapter the writer of Proverbs speaks of walking in the wise path and the wise way and of not going into the way of the wicked or straying into the company of evil people. Similarly, the first Psalm speaks of the blessed man as the one "who does not walk in the counsel of the wicked, nor stand in the path of sinners, nor sit in the seat of scoffers" (v. 1).

The idea of walking carefully and accurately in God's way is the theme of John Bunyan's *Pilgrim's Progress*. Every incident, conversation, and observation in that great classic of Christian literature focuses on obeying or disobeying, heeding or ignoring, following or departing from God's divine path for Christian living.

When I was a young boy I once walked across a narrow stream on a log that had numerous small branches sticking out of it. When a friend called to me I was momentarily distracted and tripped on one of the branches. I was already past the water and I fell into a bush of nettles on the shore. Because I had on only a swim suit, I was scratched rather painfully and the plant's microscopic needles were embedded over a large part of my body. That is a picture of what can happen to a believer when He is distracted from God's way.

When Christians sin and fall into Satan's traps, they do so because they live as unwise men rather than as wise. They revert to following the wisdom of their old lives, which was really foolishness. "For we also once were foolish ourselves," Paul said, "disobedient, deceived, enslaved to various lusts and pleasures, spending our life in malice and envy, hateful, hating one another" (Titus 3:3). God's wisdom has come to separate us from that kind of living.

"When the kindness of God our Savior and His love for mankind appeared, He saved us, not on the basis of deeds which we have done in righteousness, but according to His mercy, by the washing of regeneration and renewing by the Holy Spirit, whom He poured out upon us richly through Jesus Christ our Savior" (vv. 4–6). Our change in relationship to God is meant to bring a change in daily living, as Paul went on to explain to Titus: "Concerning these things I want you to speak confidently, so that those who have believed God will be careful to engage in good deeds. These things are good and profitable for men" (v. 8).

After David had twice spared his life, the jealous and hypocritical King Saul confessed that he had "played the fool and [had] committed a serious error" in seeking to take David's life (1 Sam. 26:21). Some years later, after David himself had become king, he proudly decided to take a census of his people. But "David's heart troubled him after he had numbered the people. So David said to the Lord, 'I have sinned greatly in what I have done. But now, O Lord, please take away the iniquity of Your servant, for I have acted very foolishly'" (2 Sam. 24:10).

. . . Lest You Fall into Foolishness

As we learn from David and from many others in Scripture, believers are not immune from reverting to foolishness. The first way a believer plays the fool is by not believing God completely. He believes God for salvation but does not continue to believe Him in and for everything else. Jesus told the two disheartened disciples on the road to Emmaus, "O foolish men and slow of heart to believe in all that the prophets have spoken" (Luke 24:25). To the extent that we do not accept any part of God's Word, to that extent we are foolish.

A believer also plays the fool when he is disobedient. "You foolish Galatians," Paul said; "who has bewitched you, before whose eyes Jesus Christ was publicly portrayed as crucified? . . . Are you so foolish? Having begun by the Spirit, are you now being perfected by the flesh?" (Gal. 3:1, 3). By failing to hold firmly to the doctrine of salvation by faith alone, the Galatians fell prey to the heresy that a Gentile must become a ceremonial Jew before he could become a Christian.

Believers also play the fool when they put their hearts on the wrong things. Paul told Timothy, for example, that "those who want to get rich fall into temptation and a snare and many foolish and harmful desires which plunge men into ruin and destruction" (1 Tim. 6:9). It is tragic that so many Christians foolishly do not take God at His word in everything He says, do not obey Him in everything He commands, and desire so many things that He warns against. There is no excuse for Christians to live foolishly when God's wisdom belongs to them. "If anyone is willing to do His will, he will know of the teaching, whether it is of God," Jesus said to the Jews (John 7:17). The Christian who genuinely wants to know God's truth will never be in doubt, either. He has all the resources he needs "to be wise in what is good, and innocent in what is evil" (Rom. 16:19).

Many people in the world are fanatically dedicated to an ideology, a religion, or a fad. The devoted communist sacrifices everything for the party. The cult follower will give all his earnings to his guru. The physical fitness enthusiast will never miss an exercise class or eat an extra calorie. By means of incredible self-discipline, men and women seeking acceptance with their deities have trained themselves to walk on beds of coals and lie on beds of nails as evidence of their religious commitment.

But not all devote themselves to false gods. Some years ago I met a recently converted young woman who was a nationally ranked distance runner. To keep in shape she ran fifteen miles a day. A month or so later she came up to me after a morning worship service and asked if I remembered her. She seemed familiar but had changed so much during that brief time that I did not recognize her. She told me who she was and explained that she had contracted a disease that the doctors had not yet been able to diagnose and that left her barely able to walk. Rather than being discouraged, however, she said that she was determined to channel the discipline that had made her such a fine athlete into discipline for the things of the Lord. That is the mark of a wise Christian.

THE BELIEVER'S LIMITED PRIVILEGES

making the most of your time, because the days are evil. (5:16)

It is common not to finish what we begin. Sometimes a symphony is unfinished, a painting uncompleted, or a project left half done because the musician, painter, or worker dies. But usually it is simply the death of a person's commitment that causes the incompletion. Dreams never become reality and hopes never materialize because those working toward them never get beyond the first few steps. For many people, including many Christians, life can be a series of unfinished symphonies. Even in the familiar opportunities of everyday Christian living, those who are truly productive have mastered the use of the hours and days of their lives.

Whether in the artistic, business, personal, or spiritual realm, no one can turn a dream into reality or fully take advantage of opportunity apart from "making the most of [his] time."

Paul did not here use *chronos*, the term for clock time, the continuous time that is measured in hours, minutes, and seconds. He rather used *kairos*, which denotes a measured, allocated, fixed season or epoch. The idea of a fixed period is also seen in the use of the definite article in the Greek text, which refers to *the* time, a concept often found in Scripture (cf. Ex. 9:5; 1 Peter 1:17). God has set boundaries to our lives, and our opportunity for service exists only within those boundaries. It is significant that the Bible speaks of such times being shortened, but never of their being lengthened. A person may die or lose an opportunity before the end of God's time, but he has no reason to expect his life or his opportunity to continue after the end of his predetermined time.

Maximizing Our Time

Having sovereignly bounded our lives with eternity, God knows both the beginning and end of our time on earth. As believers we can achieve our potential in His service only as we maximize the time He has given us, by "making the most of [our] time."

A statue near the stadium of ancient Olympia depicted Kairos (Caerus), the ancient Greek god of opportunity, said to be the youngest son of Zeus.[4] Shaped by Lysippus, a fourth-century B.C. sculptor, Kairos was depicted as a man with wings on his feet, a large lock of hair on the front of his head, and no hair at all on the back. Beneath was the inscription: "Who made thee? Lysippus made me. What is thy name? My name is Opportunity. Why hast thou wings on thy feet? That I may fly away swiftly. Why hast thou a great forelock? That men may seize me when I come. Why art thou bald in back? That when I am gone by, none can lay hold of me."

Exagorazō ("making the most of") has the basic meaning of buying, especially of buying back or buying out. It was used of buying a slave in order to set him free; thus the idea of redemption is implied in this verse. We are to redeem, buy up, all the time that we have and devote it to the Lord. The Greek is in the middle voice, indicating that we are to buy the time up for ourselves—for our own use but in the Lord's service.

Paul pleads for us to make the most of our time immediately after he pleads for us to walk wisely rather than foolishly. Outside of purposeful disobedience of God's Word, the most spiritually foolish thing a Christian can do is to waste time and opportunity, to fritter away his life in trivia and in half-hearted service of the Lord.

Shakespeare wrote,

There is a tide in the affairs of men,
Which, taken at the flood, leads on to fortune;
Omitted, all the voyage of their life
Is bound in shallows and in miseries.
(*Julius Caesar*, 4.3.217)

Napoleon said, "There is in the midst of every great battle a ten- to fifteen-minute period that is the crucial point. Take that period and you win the battle; lose it and you will be defeated."

When we walk obediently in the narrow way of the gospel, we walk carefully, making the most of our time. We take full advantage of every opportunity to serve God, redeeming our time to use for His glory. We take every opportunity to shun sin and to follow righteousness. "So then," Paul said, "while we have opportunity, let us do good to all people, and especially to those who are of the household of the faith" (Gal. 6:10).

For His own reasons, God allows some of His children to live and serve far into old age. Others He grants only a few years or even a few weeks. But none of us knows how long or short his own allocation of time will be.

When I was a boy I had a friend who, like myself, planned to be a pastor. He often told me of his plans to finish high school, go to college and seminary, and enter the pastorate. But in the twelfth grade my friend was driving his canvas-top coupe down a street and the brakes suddenly locked, catapulting him through the car top and onto the street. He struck his head against the curb and was killed instantly.

The great sixteenth-century reformer Philipp Melanchthon

kept a record of every wasted moment and took his list to God in confession at the end of each day. It is small wonder that God used him in such great ways.

Many biblical texts stand as warning beacons to those who think they will always have time to do what they should. Two of the most notable are of Noah's ark and Jesus' parable of the five foolish virgins. When Noah and his family entered the ark and shut the door, the opportunity for any other person to be saved from the flood was gone. The five foolish virgins who let their oil run out before the bridegroom came were shut out from the wedding feast (Matt. 25:8–10).

"We must work the works of Him who sent Me as long as it is day," Jesus said; "night is coming when no man can work" (John 9:4). To the unbelieving Pharisees He said, "I go away, and you will seek Me, and will die in your sin; where I am going, you cannot come" (John 8:21). After centuries of God's offering His grace to Israel, Jesus lamented, "Jerusalem, Jerusalem, who kills the prophets and stones those who are sent to her! How often I wanted to gather your children together, the way a hen gathers her chicks under her wings, and you were unwilling" (Matt. 23:37). Judas, the most tragic example of wasted opportunity, spent three years in the very presence of the Son of God, as one of the inner circle of disciples, yet he betrayed His Lord and forfeited his soul for thirty pieces of silver.

Recognizing Our Short Time on Earth

Peter said, "If you address as Father the One who impartially judges according to each one's work, conduct yourselves in fear during the time of your stay on earth" (1 Peter 1:17). In his farewell remarks to the Ephesian elders at Miletus, Paul said, "I do not consider my life of any account as dear to myself, so that I may finish my course and the ministry which I received from the Lord Jesus" (Acts 20:24). Paul's course was prescribed by God, and within that course he would minister to the utmost until his last breath. He was determined to run with endurance the race that was set before him (see Heb. 12:1). At the end of his life he therefore could say, "I have fought the good fight, I have finished the course, I have kept the faith" (2 Tim. 4:7).

David had a great awareness of time. He prayed, "How long, O Lord? Will You hide Yourself forever? . . . Remember what my span of life is" (Ps. 89:46–47). In the midst of his distress, anxiety, and pain he felt diverted from what he ought to be doing and deserted by God. He therefore asked God how long he would be sidetracked. He knew that he would live for only so long and that whatever he did for the Lord would have to be done during that time. On another occasion he prayed, "Lord, make me to know my end and what is the extent of my days; let me know how transient I am. Behold, You have made my days as handbreadths, and my lifetime as nothing in Your sight" (Ps. 39:4–5).

Paul spoke to the Corinthians about the time having been shortened (1 Cor. 7:29), and James warned, "Come now, you who say, 'Today or tomorrow we will go to such and such a city, and spend a year there and engage in business and make a profit.' Yet you do not know what your life will be like tomorrow. You are just a vapor that appears for a little while and then vanishes away" (James 4:13–14).

Kefa Sempangi was a national pastor in Africa and barely escaped with his family from brutal oppression and terror in his home country of Uganda.[5] They made their way to Philadelphia, where a group of Christians began caring for them. One day his wife said, "Tomorrow I am going to go and buy some clothes for the children," and immediately she and her husband broke into tears. Because of the constant threat of death under which they had so long lived, that was the first time in many years they had dared even speak the word *tomorrow*.

Their terrifying experiences forced them to realize what is true of every person: there is no assurance of tomorrow. The only time we can be sure of having is what we have at the moment. To the self-satisfied farmer who had grandiose plans to build bigger and better barns to store his crops, the Lord said, "You fool! This very night your soul is required of you" (Luke 12:20). He had already lived his last tomorrow.

The experience of that African family also dramatically points up the truth that "the days are evil." We are to make the most of our opportunities not only because our days are numbered but because the world continually opposes us and seeks to hinder our work for the Lord. We have little time and much opposition.

Because "the days are evil," our opportunities for freely doing righteousness are often limited. When we have opportunity to do something for His name's sake and for His glory, we should do so with all that we have. How God's heart must be broken to see His children ignore or halfheartedly take up opportunity after opportunity that He sends to them. Every moment of every day should be filled with things good, things righteous, things glorifying to God.

Falling Prey or Staying Faithful

By "the days are evil" Paul may have specifically had in mind the corrupt and debauched living that characterized the city of Ephesus. The Christians there were surrounded by paganism and infiltrated by heresy (see 4:14). Greediness, dishonesty, and immorality were a way of life in Ephesus, a way in which most of the believers had themselves once been involved and to which they were tempted to revert (4:19–32; 5:3–8).

Less than a hundred years after Paul wrote the Ephesian epistle, Rome was persecuting Christians with growing intensity and cruelty. Believers were burned alive, thrown to wild beasts, and brutalized in countless other ways. For the Ephesian church the evil times were going to become more and more evil. Several decades after Paul wrote this epistle, the Lord commended the church at Ephesus for its good works, perseverance, and resistance to false teaching. "But I have this against you," He continued, "that you have left your first love" (Rev. 2:2, 4). Because the church continued to languish in its devotion to the Lord, its lampstand was removed, as He had warned it would be if the believers there failed to "repent and do the deeds [they] did at first" (v. 5). Sometime during the second century the church in Ephesus disappeared, and there has never been a congregation there since. Because the church at Ephesus did not heed Paul's advice and the Lord's own specific warning, it ceased to exist. Instead of helping redeem the evil days in which it existed, the church fell prey to them.

If a sense of urgency was necessary in the days of the apostles, how much more is it necessary today, when we are so much nearer the Lord's return and the end of opportunity (see Rom. 13:11–14)?

When Pastor Sempangi, mentioned above, began ministering at his church in Uganda, growth was small but steady. Idi Amin had come into military and political power, and the people expected conditions in their country to improve. But soon friends and neighbors, especially those who were Christians, began to disappear. One day Pastor Sempangi visited the home of a family and found their young son standing just inside the doorway, a glazed looked on his face and his arms transfixed in the air. They discovered he had been in that state of rigid shock for days, after being forced to witness the inexpressibly brutal murder and dismembering of everyone else in his family.

Faced with a totally unexpected and horrible danger, Pastor Sempangi's church immediately realized that life as they had known it was at an end, and that the very existence of the Lord's people and the Lord's work in their land was threatened with extinction. They began continuous vigils of prayer, taking turns praying for long hours at a time. When they were not praying they were witnessing to their neighbors and friends, urging them to receive Christ and be saved.

The church in Uganda stands today, and it has not died. In many ways it is stronger than ever. Its lampstand is still very much in place and shining brightly for the Lord, because His people made the most of the time, did not succumb to the evil days in which they lived, and would not leave their first love. It cost many of them dearly, but they proved again that the blood of the martyrs is the seed of the church.

THE LORD'S PURPOSES

So then do not be foolish, but understand what the will of the Lord is. (5:17)

"Do not be foolish" repeats and reinforces Paul's previous plea for believers not to be unwise, and "understand what the will of the Lord is" expands and makes more explicit his plea to walk wisely (v. 15).

In light of the urgency to make the most of our time, not being foolish includes, among other things, not becoming anxious or panicked. When we look around at the pervasiveness of evil and at the unending needs for evangelism and service to others in Christ's name, it is easy to be overwhelmed. We are tempted either to give up and withdraw or to become hyperactive, losing precision, purpose, and effectiveness in a frenzy of superficial activity.

The proper sense of urgency, however, drives the wise believer to want more than ever to "understand what the will of the Lord is," because he knows that only in the Lord's will and power can anything good and lasting be accomplished. He will not be foolish by running frenetically in every direction trying to see how many programs and projects he can become involved in. Such activity easily becomes futile and can lead to burnout and discouragement, because it works in the power of the flesh even when it is well-intentioned. Trying to run ahead of God only puts us further behind in His work.

The work of many churches would be greatly strengthened if the number of its superfluous programs and activities were cut back and the Lord's will was sought more carefully and the principles of His Word applied more faithfully. When our priorities are God's priorities, He is free to work in us and through us to accomplish great things; but when our priorities are not His priorities He can do little with us because He has little of us.

The unwise believers who behave in a foolish manner try to function apart from God's will and are inevitably weak, frustrated, and ineffective, both in their personal lives and in their work for God. The only cure for such foolishness is to find and to follow the will of the Lord.

God's basic will is, of course, found in Scripture. Here we find His perfect and sufficient guidelines for knowing and doing what is pleasing to Him. But the will of which Paul seems to be speaking here is the Lord's specific leading of individual believers. Although

His plans and directions for each believer are not found in Scripture, the general principles for understanding them are there. God does not promise to show us His will through visions, strange coincidences, or miracles. Nor does He play a divine guessing game with us, seeing if we can somehow stumble onto His will like a small child finds an egg at an Easter egg hunt. God's deepest desire for all of His children is that they know and obey His will, and He gives us every possible help both to know and to obey it.

God's will for our lives is first of all to belong to Him through Jesus Christ. His first and primary will for every person is that he be saved and brought into the family and kingdom of God (1 Tim. 2:3–4). God's will is also that we be Spirit-filled. As Paul went on to teach in the following verse, we are not to "get drunk with wine, for that is dissipation, but be filled with the Spirit" (Eph. 5:18).

We experience God's will by being sanctified. "This is the will of God, your sanctification" (1 Thess. 4:3), Paul said. And we enjoy His will through proper submission to other men. "Submit yourselves for the Lord's sake to every human institution, whether to a king as the one in authority, or to governors as sent by him for the punishment of evildoers and the praise of those who do right. For such is the will of God that by doing right you may silence the ignorance of foolish men" (1 Peter 2:13–15). Likewise we are to be submissive to leaders in the church: "Obey your leaders and submit to them, for they keep watch over your souls as those who will give an account" (Heb. 13:17).

God's will may include suffering. "If when you do what is right and suffer for it you patiently endure it, this finds favor with God" (1 Peter 2:20; cf. 3:17; 5:10). God's will culminates in believers' giving thanks no matter what. "In everything give thanks; for this is God's will for you in Christ Jesus" (1 Thess. 5:18).

When a person is saved, sanctified, submissive, suffering, and thankful, he is already *in* God's will. "Delight yourself in the Lord; and He will give you the desires of your heart" (Ps. 37:4), David tells us. In other words, when we are who God wants us to be, He is in control and our will is merged with His will, and He therefore gives us the desires He has planted in our hearts.

Jesus is our supreme example for fulfilling the commands of Ephesians 5:15–17. He always functioned according to the divine principles established by His Father: "Truly, truly, I say to you, the Son can do nothing of Himself, unless it is something He sees the Father doing; for whatever the Father does, these things the Son also does in like manner" (John 5:19; cf. v. 30). Second, Jesus knew that His time of earthly ministry was short and would soon be cut off, as seen in frequent sayings such as "My time has not yet come" and "My time has come." He always functioned according to His limited privilege of time and opportunity, using every moment of His life in His Father's work. Third, Jesus always functioned according to the His Father's purposes. "My food is to do the will of Him who sent Me and to accomplish His work" (John 4:34).

"Therefore," Peter said, "since Christ has suffered in the flesh, arm yourselves also with the same purpose, because he who has suffered in the flesh has ceased from sin, so as to live the rest of the time in the flesh no longer for the lusts of men, but for the will of God" (1 Peter 4:1–2).

The words of David sum up the proper reaction to this teaching: "I will sing of mercy and judgment: unto thee, O Lord, will I sing. I will behave myself wisely in a perfect way" (Ps. 101:1–2 KJV).

Chapter 8

---◦∽◦---

WALKING
IN THE TRUTH

2 JOHN 1–4

The elder to the chosen lady and her children, whom I love in truth; and not only I, but also all who know the truth, for the sake of the truth which abides in us and will be with us forever: Grace, mercy and peace will be with us, from God the Father and from Jesus Christ, the Son of the Father, in truth and love. I was very glad to find some of your children walking in truth, just as we have received commandment to do from the Father. (1–4)

When Pilate asked cynically, "What is truth?" (John 18:38), he reflected the view of many today. Postmodernism regards the concept of truth with skepticism. Many believe that there is no such thing as absolute truth or, if there is, that it cannot be known. Certainly, they argue, there is no religious truth; religion is merely a personal preference, like one's taste in art, music, or literature.

But truth—absolute, divine truth—*does* exist, and it is the most important reality in the universe. When Martha complained that her sister was not helping her with the serving, Jesus replied, "Martha, Martha, you are worried and bothered about so many things; but only one thing is necessary, for Mary has chosen the good part, which shall not be taken away from her" (Luke 10:41–42). There was no higher priority than for Mary to be "seated at the Lord's feet, listening to His word" of truth (v. 39).

Truth is a precious commodity, more valuable than any earthly riches (cf. Pss. 119:72, 127); once found, it is to be held on to at all costs. Thus Proverbs 23:23 exhorts, "Buy truth, and do not sell it."

THE BIBLE AND THE THEME OF TRUTH

The Bible, the word of truth (Ps. 119:160; John 17:17; 2 Cor. 6:7; 2 Tim. 2:15; James 1:18), majors on the theme of truth. God is the "God of truth" (Ps. 31:5; Isa. 65:16), who abounds in truth (Ex. 34:6) and always speaks the truth (2 Sam. 7:28; cf. Num. 23:19; Titus 1:2); Christ is the truth (John 14:6; Eph. 4:21), is full of truth (John 1:14), revealed the truth (John 1:17), spoke the truth (John 8:45–46), and testified to the truth (John 18:37); the Holy Spirit is the Spirit of truth (John 14:17; 15:26; 16:13; 1 John 5:6). God's truth is eternal (Ps. 117:2), infinite (Pss. 57:10; 86:15; 108:4), and saving (Ps. 69:13).

Further, salvation comes from faith in the truth (2 Thess. 2:13; cf. 1 Tim. 2:4; 2 Tim. 2:25). Believers are sanctified by the truth (John 17:17), love the truth (cf. 2 Thess. 2:10), are set free by the truth (John 8:32), worship in the truth (John 4:23–24), rejoice in the truth (1 Cor. 13:6), speak the truth (Eph. 4:15, 25), meditate on the truth (Phil. 4:8), manifest the truth (2 Cor. 4:2), obey the truth (1 Peter 1:22), are guided by the truth (Pss. 25:5; 43:3) and, most comprehensively, walk in the truth (1 Kings 2:4; 3:6; 2 Kings 20:3; Pss. 26:3; 86:11).

Believers must be committed to the truth, because we exist in the world, which is the realm of Satan (1 John 5:19), the "father of lies" (John 8:44). He strives to keep sinners from understanding and believing the truth; he is "the god of this world [who] has blinded the minds of the unbelieving so that they might not see the light of the gospel of the glory of Christ, who is the image of God" (2 Cor. 4:4). As a result, "Everyone deceives his neighbor and does not speak the truth, they have taught their tongue to speak lies" (Jer. 9:5). Unbelievers are "men of depraved mind and deprived of the truth" (1 Tim. 6:5), who "oppose the truth" (2 Tim. 3:8), and "turn away their ears from the truth" (2 Tim. 4:4) because "they exchanged the truth of God for a lie" (Rom. 1:25).

The Church and the Theme of Truth

In a world of lies, the church is called to be the "pillar and support of the truth" (1 Tim. 3:15). Paul's metaphor would have been readily understood by Timothy and his congregation at Ephesus. Located in that city was the temple of Diana (Artemis; Acts 19:23–28), one of the Seven Wonders of the Ancient World. The temple's immense roof was supported by 127 pillars, which rested on a massive foundation. Just as that temple was a monument to the lies of Satan, so the church is to be a testimony to the truth of God. The church's mission is to immovably, unshakably live, uphold, and proclaim the truth of God's Word. It is to proclaim the "whole purpose of God" (Acts 20:27), not merely that part of divine truth that is inoffensive to the surrounding culture. In the words of Martin Luther, a stalwart champion of necessary controversy,

> If I profess with the loudest voice and clearest exposition every portion of the truth of God except precisely that little point which the

187

world and the devil are at that moment attacking, I am not *confessing* Christ, however boldly I may be *professing* Christ. Where the battle rages, there the loyalty of the soldier is proved, and to be steady on all the battlefield besides, is mere flight and disgrace if he flinches at that point.[1]

Any so-called church that fails to exercise its stewardship of His truth faces God's judgment—just as the Jews did for failing to uphold and live the Old Testament truth entrusted to them (cf. Rom. 2:23–24). But throughout its history, the true church has clung tenaciously to the truth, despite the storms of persecution, the sting of rejection, and the assaults of enemies both from inside and outside its ranks (cf. Acts 20:29–30). And countless thousands have suffered martyrdom rather than compromise or abandon the truth.

Strategically, the final epistles of the New Testament, Second and Third John, emphasize the priority of truth and the need to contend for it in the face of apostate liars (described by Jude).

John wrote the two brief epistles of Second and Third John— more postcards than letters—to stress the importance of truth. *Alētheia* ("truth") appears five times in this opening section of Second John and six times in Third John. Though each is a personal letter to an individual, John was writing about the inspired revelation of God that was to God's people throughout time. Recognizing that all the readers of his letter faced and always would face a world of lies and deceit, he wrote to call them to live in God's truth, to love within the bounds of truth, and to be loyal to and look out for the truth. In the opening verses John reveals four features of walking in the truth: the truth unites, indwells, blesses, and controls believers.

THE TRUTH UNITES BELIEVERS

The elder to the chosen lady and her children, whom I love in truth; and not only I, but also all who know the truth, (1)

By the time he wrote this epistle, John was a very old man, the last surviving apostle. Even so, his reference to himself as "the elder" (*presbuteros* with the definite article) stresses not so much his age as his position of spiritual oversight for the church. In the New Testament the term, borrowing from familiar Old Testament usage (cf. Lev. 4:15; Num. 11:25; Deut. 25:7–8, etc.), generally refers to the office of elder (the exception is in 1 Tim. 5:1, where it refers simply to an older man); the related term *presbutēs* (translated "old man" in Luke 1:18 and "aged" in Philem. 9) describes an older man without reference to a leadership role. John's description of himself reinforces the truth that he wrote this epistle; someone impersonating him would likely have chosen the title "apostle," while a writer not trying to impersonate him would not likely have called himself *the* elder.[2] John did not need to refer to himself as an apostle because his readers knew and accepted him as such, though in the experience of the church, he served them as their pastor.

In the New Testament, churches were always taught and ruled by a plurality of elders (Acts 11:30; 14:23; 15:2, 4, 6, 22, 23; 16:4; 20:17; 21:18; 1 Tim. 5:17; Titus 1:5; James 5:14; 1 Peter 5:1, 5). But though there were other elders serving with John in Ephesus (cf. Acts 20:17), he was the patriarchal elder, whose authority and oversight extended well beyond Ephesus. Like Peter (1 Peter 5:1), John was both an elder and an apostle; as the last of the apostles, he was *the* elder, the most distinguished of all elders; the only living elder who was chosen to be an apostle by the Lord Jesus Christ and was a member of the innermost circle of the twelve apostles; the one singled out as the "disciple whom Jesus loved" (John 20:2; cf. 13:23; 19:26; 21:7, 20). In contrast to the false teachers, John was the torchbearer of apostolic tradition.

The "chosen lady" to whom John addressed this letter was an actual woman, not a church. "Lady" translates the feminine form of the noun *kurios* ("lord," "sir"). The husband is the "lord" of the household as its divinely ordained head (cf. 1 Cor. 11:3; Eph. 5:23), but the lady has her sphere of authority and responsibility as well (cf. 1 Tim. 5:14; "keep house" translates a Greek verb that literally means, "to rule or manage a household"). That her husband is not mentioned may indicate that she was a widow. In any case, she was responsible for providing hospitality in the home, as is clear from 1 Timothy 5:10. Since John addressed her children too, they may still have been living at home with her. Families typically shared a common house, even after the children were married.

John's description of this woman (and her sister; v. 13) as "chosen"—from the Greek *eklektos* ("elect," "chosen," "choice")— reflects the biblical truth that God sovereignly chooses believers for salvation (Matt. 22:14; 24:22, 24, 31; Mark 13:20, 22, 27; Luke 18:7; Rom. 8:33; Col. 3:12; 2 Tim. 2:10; Titus 1:1; 1 Peter 1:1; 2:9; 2 John 13; Rev. 17:14).[3] Unlike those who hold a weak view of divine sovereignty, the New Testament writers did not hesitate to refer to believers as "the elect." In fact, the Lord Jesus Christ Himself did so in Matthew 24:22: "Unless those days had been cut short, no life would have been saved; but for the sake of the elect those days will be cut short." The term is no less appropriate than the more popular terms "child of God," "saved," "born again," "believer," or "Christian."

John's statement "whom I love in truth" reveals his personal connection to this family (the relative pronoun *hous* ["whom"] is plural and encompasses both the lady and her children). *Egō* ("I") is emphatic, stressing the apostle's personal, ongoing (the verb is in the present tense) love for them. The love in view here is that willful, spiritual devotion and service conveyed by the familiar verb *agapaō*. The phrase "in truth" explains and qualifies John's love for them. It does not refer to his sincerity; he was not merely claiming to "truly" love them, though he obviously did. Rather, "truth" refers here to the embodiment of truth in the gospel. It is parallel to the frequent New Testament expression "the faith" (Acts 6:7; 13:8; 14:22; 16:5; 1 Cor. 16:13; 2 Cor. 13:5; Gal. 1:23; Eph. 4:13; Phil. 1:27; Col. 1:23; 1 Tim. 1:2; 3:9; 4:1; 5:8; 6:10, 21; 2 Tim. 3:8; Titus 1:13; Jude 3).

John's expression is similar to Paul's exhortation to Titus, "Greet those who love us in the faith" (Titus 3:15); that is, in the objective truth of the gospel. It was the truth that bound not only John, but also all who knew the truth to this lady and her children. It is their common belief in the gospel truth that unites all believers.

John's statement encapsulates the main theme of this brief epistle, that truth must always govern the exercise of love. Christians' deep, mutual affection flows out of their shared commitment to the truth. In his first epistle John wrote, "Whoever believes that Jesus is the Christ is born of God, and whoever loves the Father loves the child born of Him" (1 John 5:1). We can have no real communion with those who reject the truth of the gospel, since we share no common spiritual life with them. Such people are outside the fellowship of believers, because it is only those who "have in obedience to the truth purified [their] souls" who can have "a sincere love of the brethren" (1 Peter 1:22).

Because salvation requires belief in the truth, it is critically important for the church to proclaim the right message. A simple, accurate presentation of the gospel is sufficient, through the transforming power of the Holy Spirit, to bring about salvation. On the other hand, the most carefully crafted, smoothly polished presentation of anything less than the gospel will not save.

John's linking of love and truth shows that they are anything but incompatible, as some are always eager to suggest. Believers are to speak in love, but they are also to speak the truth (Eph. 4:15). To minimize the truth in the name of love is to abandon biblical love, which is based on the truth. God's purposes will never be accomplished by compromising His truth; love for souls is never manifested by minimizing the truth.

THE TRUTH INDWELLS BELIEVERS

for the sake of the truth which abides in us and will be with us forever: (2)

In keeping with his passionate commitment to the truth, John wrote this epistle "for the sake of the truth." His concern was that the Christian lady to whom he addressed it might compromise truth in the name of hospitality. Christian love, fellowship, and hospitality are vitally important, since they manifest the transforming power of the gospel (cf. Rom. 12:13; 1 Tim. 3:2; Titus 1:8; 1 Peter 4:9). Believers share a spiritual love that flows from their common eternal life in Christ. But they cannot genuinely manifest that love apart from an unswerving commitment to the truth of God's Word. That truth permeates all aspects of the church's individual and corporate life, underlying all of its preaching, evangelism, and fellowship.

In language reminiscent of Jesus' promise concerning the Holy Spirit (John 14:17), John wrote that the "truth . . . abides in us and will be with us forever." The parallel is appropriate, since the Holy

Spirit is the "Spirit of truth" (John 14:17; 15:26; 16:13; 1 John 5:6). Though in a lifetime we cannot comprehend the vast depth of all biblical truth, all true Christians know the truth of the Scripture that saves. They know that they are sinners, facing God's just judgment, and that forgiveness comes only through faith in the Lord Jesus Christ and His atoning sacrifice and resurrection. If they did not comprehend those facts, they would not be Christians since, as noted above, understanding the truth is necessary for salvation.

In his first epistle, John taught that all believers are able to discern the truth from error:

> You have an anointing from the Holy One, and you all know. I have not written to you because you do not know the truth, but because you do know it. . . . As for you, the anointing which you received from Him abides in you, and you have no need for anyone to teach you; but as His anointing teaches you about all things, and is true and is not a lie, and just as it has taught you, you abide in Him. (1 John 2:20–21, 27)

Menō ("abides") is one of John's favorite terms, appearing more than sixty times in his writings. It is used in a theological sense to refer to the truth that resides in believers (1 John 2:13, 24; cf. John 5:38 where Jesus upbraids the unbelieving Jews for not having the Word abiding in them), to true believers abiding in the Word (John 8:31) and thus not being in spiritual darkness (John 12:46), to the Spirit abiding in believers (John 14:17; cf. 1 John 4:12, 15, 16) and, most significant, to believers abiding in Christ (John 6:56; 14:10; 15:4–7, 9–10; 1 John 2:6, 10, 28; 3:6, 24; 4:13). The truth of the Word, which "abides in [believers] . . . forever," gives them "the mind of Christ" (1 Cor. 2:16).

The Truth Blesses Believers

Grace, mercy and peace will be with us, from God the Father and from Jesus Christ, the Son of the Father, in truth and love. (3)

Although the three words appear together only here and in Paul's letters to Timothy (1 Tim. 1:2; 2 Tim. 1:2), *grace*, *mercy*, and *peace* are familiar New Testament terms. They are often used in the salutations of the epistles. *Grace* combines with *peace* in Romans 1:7, 1 Corinthians 1:3, 2 Corinthians 1:2, Galatians 1:3, Ephesians 1:2, Philippians 1:2, Colossians 1:2, 1 Thessalonians 1:1, 2 Thessalonians 1:2, Titus 1:4, Philemon 3, 1 Peter 1:2, 2 Peter 1:2, and Revelation 1:4; *mercy* with *peace* in Jude 2. The three terms summarize the progression of the plan of salvation: God's grace caused Him to grant mercy, which results in peace. Grace views sinners as guilty and undeserving (Rom. 5:20; Eph. 1:7); mercy views them as needy and helpless (Matt. 5:3; Rom. 11:30–32; Eph. 2:4–5; Titus 3:5; 1 Peter 1:3); peace is the result of God's outpouring of both (Acts 10:36; Rom. 5:1; Eph. 2:14; Col. 1:20). These divine blessings, like everything in the Christian life, come only from "God the Father and from Jesus Christ, the Son of the Father." From God, "the Father of lights, with whom there is no variation or shifting shadow" comes down "every good thing given and every perfect gift" (James 1:17). And through the Son, all "the promises of God . . . are yes" (2 Cor. 1:20). They are present when believers allow divine truth to dominate the mind and heart, resulting in genuine love.

The Truth Controls Believers

I was very glad to find some of your children walking in truth, just as we have received commandment to do from the Father. (4)

In light of his commitment to the truth, it comes as no surprise that John "was very glad to find some" of this Christian lady's "children walking in truth." Surely the apostle was exuberant at the news of their obedience to divine revelation, which he may have heard from her sister or her sister's children (cf. v. 13). That he mentions only some of her children does not necessarily mean that the others were not saved; John was referring only to those of whom he had personal knowledge.

The truth of God's Word is to be lived as well as believed (cf. Matt. 7:21; 12:50; Luke 6:46–49; 11:28; John 13:17; Rom. 2:13; James 1:22; 1 John 2:3). The phrase "walking in truth" refers to moving through life controlled by the truth; it is the equivalent to walking in the light (1 John 1:7). "Walking" is a frequent New Testament metaphor for the Christian life. Believers "walk in newness of life" (Rom. 6:4), "walk by faith, not by sight" (2 Cor. 5:7), "walk by the Spirit" (Gal. 5:16, 25), walk in good works (Eph. 2:10), "walk in a manner worthy of the calling with which [they] have been called" (Eph. 4:1), "walk in love" (Eph. 5:2), "walk as children of Light" (Eph. 5:8), walk in wisdom (Eph. 5:15). They are to "walk in a manner worthy of the Lord, to please Him in all respects" (Col. 1:10), "walk in a manner worthy of the God who calls [them] into His own kingdom and glory" (1 Thess. 2:12), "walk in the same manner as [Jesus] walked" (1 John 2:6), and "walk according to His commandments" (2 John 6).

John's reference to the commandment believers have received from the Father to walk in the truth is not a reference to one particular command, but reflects the general and obvious mandate of Scripture to obey. Scripture is even called "the commandment of the Lord" (Ps. 19:8; cf. the similar use of "commandment" in 1 Tim. 6:14). Obedience to God's truth is not optional. "God has not revealed His truth in such a way as to leave us free at our pleasure to believe or disbelieve it, to obey or disobey it. Revelation carries with it responsibility, and the clearer the revelation, the greater the responsibility to believe and obey it (cf. Am. iii.2)"[4]

This brief letter opens with a ringing call for Christians to live consistently with the truth they believe. The only true basis for unity in the church is the truth of God's Word that indwells, blesses, and controls the lives of individual believers. And it is only those Christians and churches who are firmly planted on the solid foundation of the truth who will be able to withstand the storms of persecution, temptation, and false doctrine that constantly assail them.

—∞—

Chapter 9

WALKING BY FAITH

2 Corinthians 5:6–10

Therefore, being always of good courage, and knowing that while we are at home in the body we are absent from the Lord— for we walk by faith, not by sight—we are of good courage, I say, and prefer rather to be absent from the body and to be at home with the Lord. Therefore we also have as our ambition, whether at home or absent, to be pleasing to Him. For we must all appear before the judgment seat of Christ, so that each one may be recompensed for his deeds in the body, according to what he has done, whether good or bad. (5:6–10)

As he wrote this letter to the Corinthian church, Paul was facing death on a daily basis. Hostility swirled around him, animosity was constant, and so was the reality and threat of opposition and terminal persecution. Both unbelieving Jews and Gentiles sought to take his life, viewing him as a danger to their religion (cf. Acts 13:50; 18:13), their economic prosperity (cf. Acts 19:23–27), and even to their political stability (cf. Acts 17:6). The apostle's sense of imminent death comes through repeatedly in this epistle:

For we do not want you to be unaware, brethren, of our affliction which came to us in Asia, that we were burdened excessively, beyond our strength, so that we despaired even of life; indeed, we had the sentence of death within ourselves so that we would not trust in ourselves, but in God who raises the dead; who delivered us from so great a peril of death, and will deliver us, He on whom we have set our hope. (2 Cor. 1:8–10)

But we have this treasure in earthen vessels, so that the surpassing greatness of the power will be of God and not from ourselves; we are afflicted in every way, but not crushed; perplexed, but not despairing; persecuted, but not forsaken; struck down, but not destroyed; always carrying about in the body the dying of Jesus, so that the life of Jesus also may be manifested in our body. For we who live are constantly being delivered over to death for Jesus' sake, so that the life of Jesus also may be manifested in our mortal flesh. So death works in us, but life in you. (4:7–12)

He described his life as "dying yet behold, we live; punished yet not put to death" (6:9), and "often in danger of death" (11:23). How did he face the reality that he, like a soldier in the front lines, constantly lived on the brink of death?

Some might have expected Paul to tone down his fearless heralding of the gospel, since it was that preaching that enraged his enemies and thus jeopardized his life. Being less confrontational would have mitigated the threat he faced. But the more the hostility and persecution escalated, the bolder Paul became. He never wavered in courageously proclaiming the truth. Because he faced death confidently, even gladly, that triumphant perspective caused him to write, "For to me, to live is Christ and to die is gain. . . . I am hard-pressed from both directions, having the desire to depart and be with Christ, for that is very much better" (Phil. 1:21, 23). And because he did not fear death, Paul did not fear persecution, pain, or suffering; he was able always to be "of good courage" (2 Cor. 5:6, 8).

This passage builds on the truths Paul revealed in 4:16–5:5, when he wrote that no matter how difficult his circumstances were, he "[did] not lose heart," because "though [his] outer man [was] decaying, yet [his] inner man [was] being renewed day by day." He understood that "momentary, light affliction is producing for us an eternal weight of glory far beyond all comparison, while we look not at the things which are seen, but at the things which are not seen; for the things which are seen are temporal, but the things which are not seen are eternal" (4:17–18).

Paul was able to maintain that kind of triumphant perspective because he walked by faith, not by sight. His faith was not anchored in the riches or accolades of this life, but in the promises and purposes of his loving heavenly Father. As a result, He gladly suffered in this world for a far greater reward in the world to come.

PAUL'S HEAVENLY PERSPECTIVE

For all, death comes like an utterly unsympathetic landlord waving an eviction notice. But that eviction merely releases believers from a wretched earthly neighborhood to an infinitely grand and glorious dwelling in a heavenly neighborhood. For the believer, then, the sorrows, disappointments, and suffering of this life are worse than death. Death releases believers from the relatively dilapidated slum in which they now live and ushers them into a room in the house of the eternal Father in the heavenly city.

Knowing that, Christians should not fear death. They should long "to depart and be with Christ, for that is very much better" (Phil. 1:23). That does not mean, of course, that they are to be foolishly reckless or careless with their lives; their bodies belong to God (1 Cor. 6:19–20). But an obsessive concern for one's physical well-being or a morbid fear of death is inconsistent with a Christian perspective. Believers should long for heaven like a prisoner longs for freedom, like a sick man longs for health, like a hungry man longs for food, like a thirsty man longs for a drink, like a poor man longs for a payday, and like a soldier longs for peace. Hope and courage in facing death is the last opportunity for Christians to exhibit their faith in God, to prove their hope of heaven is genuine, and to heighten their confidence in the promises of God.

In this passage, the apostle Paul demonstrates what it means to walk by faith and not by sight, as he lives in the light of heaven's future glory. His heavenly perspective fueled both his anticipation for the next life and his ambition in this one.

PAUL'S EAGER ANTICIPATION

Therefore, being always of good courage, and knowing that while we are at home in the body we are absent from the Lord— for we walk by faith, not by sight—we are of good courage, I say, and prefer rather to be absent from the body and to be at home with the Lord. (5:6–8)

In verses 6–8 Paul reached the pinnacle of heavenly anticipation. He looked forward to his new, glorified body, the perfection of heaven, and the eternal fulfillment of God's plan. But beyond all of that was the wonderful reality that death would usher him into the presence of the Lord. "Therefore" points back to the foundational truths Paul expressed in verses 1–5. On the basis of those truths, Paul was "always of good courage" in the face of death. His courage was not a temporary feeling or a passing emotion; it was a constant state of mind. He faced death cheerfully, with complete confidence. It was not that he did not love the people in his life, but he loved the Lord more. Life for Paul was a race to finish, a battle to win, a stewardship to discharge. Once the race was over and the stewardship discharged, Paul saw no reason to cling to this life. The only reason for him to remain on earth was to serve God, and he told Timothy of his readiness to leave when that service was complete:

> For I am already being poured out as a drink offering, and the time of my departure has come. I have fought the good fight, I have finished the course, I have kept the faith; in the future there is laid up for me the crown of righteousness, which the Lord, the righteous Judge, will award to me on that day; and not only to me, but also to all who have loved His appearing. (2 Tim. 4:6–8)

The reality of life in this world for believers, however, is "that while we are at home in the body" (living in the flesh) we are just temporarily "absent from the Lord." Believers communicate with the Lord through prayer and the study of the Word and have communion with Him through the indwelling Holy Spirit. Yet there is still a sense in which they are separated from God and long for that separation to end.

Psalm 42:1–2 expresses that desire: "As the deer pants for the water brooks, so my soul pants for You, O God. My soul thirsts for God, for the living God; when shall I come and appear before God?" "Whom have I in heaven but You?" The psalmist Asaph asked rhetorically. "And besides You, I desire nothing on earth" (Ps. 73:25). Paul longed for the day when he would "always be with the Lord" (1 Thess. 4:17). That sense of separation caused Abraham to look for "the city . . . whose architect and builder is God" (Heb. 11:10) and the Old Testament saints to acknowledge "that they were strangers and exiles on the earth" (Heb. 11:13). It is only in heaven that believers will have intimate, unbroken fellowship with God (cf. Rev. 21:3–4, 22–23; 22:3–4).

The statement in verse 7 that "we walk by faith, not by sight" explains how believers can have fellowship with and serve the invisible God in this life. Such faith is not a wishful fantasy or a vague superstition but a strong confidence grounded in the truth of Scripture. It is "the assurance of things hoped for, the conviction of things not seen" (Heb. 11:1).

Then Paul adds the triumphant declaration, "We are of good courage, I say, and prefer rather to be absent from the body and to be at home with the Lord." He repeats the truth from verse 6 that he was always positive toward the future despite the constantly looming reality of death. To "prefer rather to be absent from the body and to be at home with the Lord" is to understand our temporary time on earth only as a stranger's experience and heaven as our true and permanent home.

PAUL'S EARNEST AMBITION

Therefore we also have as our ambition, whether at home or absent, to be pleasing to Him. For we must all appear before the judgment seat of Christ, so that each one may be recompensed for his deeds in the body, according to what he has done, whether good or bad. (5:9–10)

Ambition has always had a bad reputation. The noble Puritan writer Thomas Brooks wrote, "Ambition is a gilded misery, a secret poison, a hidden plague, the engineer of deceit, the mother of hypocrisy, the parent of envy, the original of vices, the moth of holiness, the blinder of hearts.... High seats are never but uneasy."[1] Blind ambition causes people to compromise their convictions, violate their beliefs, and sacrifice their character. Indeed, ambition drives people to seek wealth, prestige, power, social prominence, popular acclaim, and dominance over others.

Expressing that negative connotation of ambition, Stephen Neill said, "I am inclined to think that ambition in any ordinary sense of the term is nearly always sinful in ordinary men. I am certain that in the Christian it is always sinful, and that it is most inexcusable of all in the ordained minister."[2]

Clearly the Bible condemns sinful ambition (cf. Jer. 45:4). Yet there is a kind of ambition it sanctions: an ambition to please the Lord. Paul wrote, "We have as our ambition . . . to be pleasing to Him" (v. 9). He used the word in the positive sense of loving what is noble or honorable. In fact, the Greek word translated "have as our ambition," *philotimeomai*, is a compound word from *philos* ("love") and *time* ("honor"). It was that type of noble ambition that characterized Paul.

Significantly, Paul used *philotimeomai* only two other times in his writings (the only other times it appears in the New Testament). In Romans 15:20 he wrote, "I aspired [from *philotimeomai*] to preach the gospel, not where Christ was already named, so that I would not build on another man's foundation"; while in 1 Thessalonians 4:11 he exhorted the Thessalonians, "Make it your ambition to lead a quiet life and attend to your own business and work with your hands, just as we commanded you." The same point is made in 1 Timothy 3:1, though Paul used different Greek words: "If any man aspires [from *oregō*] to the office of overseer, it is a fine work he desires [from *epithumeō*] to do." As Paul's example demonstrates, there is a central place in the Christian life for noble ambition, for a passion for what is excellent and honorable.

PAUL'S HIGHEST GOAL

to be pleasing to Him. (9c)

Paul's earnest ambition was also his noblest goal, to be pleasing to God. In fact, the noblest and highest ambition to which anyone can aspire is to be pleasing to God. Paul used the adjective *euarestos* ("pleasing") frequently in his writings. In Romans 12:1–2 and 14:18 he used it to speak of behavior that is acceptable to God. He urged the Ephesians to try "to learn what is pleasing to the Lord" (Eph. 5:10). He described the Philippians' financial support of him as being "well-pleasing to God" (Phil. 4:18). In Colossians 3:20 he noted that children's obedience to their parents "is well-pleasing to the Lord." *Euarestos* also appears in Titus 2:9, where it describes slaves who are pleasing to their masters. Godly ambition seeks to please the Lord in all aspects of life (Col. 1:10).

Nowhere is the focus of Paul's ambition more clearly articulated than in 1 Corinthians 4:3–5. There, he writes:

> But to me it is a very small thing that I may be examined by you, or by any human court; in fact, I do not even examine myself. For I am conscious of nothing against myself, yet I am not by this acquitted; but the one who examines me is the Lord. Therefore do not go on passing judgment before the time, but wait until the Lord comes who will both bring to light the things hidden in the darkness and disclose the motives of men's hearts; and then each man's praise will come to him from God.

One of the many problems besetting the Corinthian church was that of judging others unrighteously. Its various factions (cf. 1 Cor. 1:12; 3:4) constantly sat in condemnation on each other. Even Paul was under relentless, merciless assault from some demonic self-styled false apostles at Corinth. Those false teachers attacked his apostolic credentials, his ministry methods, his character, and even the gospel message he preached.

Unperturbed by the savage onslaught against him, Paul responded, "But to me it is a very small thing that I may be examined by you, or by any human court" (1 Cor. 4:3). Their opinion of him was not important to him, because he did not seek to please men, but God. Paul viewed himself as a servant and steward of God (1 Cor. 4:1; cf. 9:17; Eph. 3:2; Col. 1:25; Titus 1:7) and therefore accountable to Him. The apostle was not concerned with earthly, biased evaluations of him (whether positive or negative); no human court, whether an official tribunal or the unofficial court of human opinion, could render the ultimate verdict on him.

Going beyond that, Paul wrote, "In fact, I do not even examine myself" (1 Cor. 4:3). He was wise enough to know that he was biased in his own favor and thus lacked objectivity. Though he was "conscious of nothing against [himself]" (v. 4; cf. 2 Cor. 1:12), Paul understood that "the heart is more deceitful than all else and is desperately sick; who can understand it?" (Jer. 17:9). Therefore he applied to himself the warning he expressed in 1 Corinthians 10:12: "Let him who thinks he stands take heed that he does not fall."

Paul's was not a brash, defiant, self-righteous attitude that refused to submit to scrutiny or judgment. Nor was he arguing that believers should not confront other believers who continue in sin (cf. 1 Cor. 5:12; 6:1–5). He was not talking about a sin issue, for he wrote that he was "conscious of nothing against [himself]" (1 Cor.

4:4). The apostle's point was that neither he nor the Corinthians were able to judge him properly; that judgment was reserved for a higher court, "because the one who examines [him] is the Lord" (v. 4).

Paul concluded his point by exhorting the Corinthians, "Therefore do not go on passing judgment before the time" (v. 5). The ultimate and accurate verdict on anyone's life and ministry will be rendered by the Lord, who when He returns "will both bring to light the things hidden in the darkness and disclose the motives of men's hearts; and then each man's praise will come to him from God" (v. 5). In light of that reality believers should "walk in a manner worthy of the Lord, to please Him in all respects" (Col. 1:10; cf. 1 Thess. 4:1). At the end of his life, Paul believed he had some measure of fulfillment of his spiritual ambition (2 Tim. 4:7–8).

PAUL'S DEVOTION WAS WITHOUT LIMITS
whether at home or absent, (9b)

Paul's devotion to his noble ambition knew no limits, as the all-encompassing phrase "whether at home or absent" indicates. That phrase connects Paul's thought with verses 6 and 8, as does the phrase "therefore also" that begins verse 9. Throughout his ministry, Paul constantly lived on the brink of death. Describing that ever-present threat earlier in the letter, the apostle wrote poignantly,

> We are afflicted in every way, but not crushed; perplexed, but not despairing; persecuted, but not forsaken; struck down, but not destroyed; always carrying about in the body the dying of Jesus, so that the life of Jesus also may be manifested in our body. For we who live are constantly being delivered over to death for Jesus' sake, so that

the life of Jesus also may be manifested in our mortal flesh. So death works in us, but life in you. (2 Cor. 4:8–12; cf. 6:9)

Because he constantly stared death in the face, Paul longed, as he wrote in 2 Corinthians 5:1, to leave his "earthly tent" (his physical body) and receive his "building from God, a house not made with hands, eternal in the heavens" (his resurrection body). Paul's first choice was to live until the Rapture, when that transformation would take place. If that was not God's will for him (as in fact it was not), Paul's second choice was "to be absent from the body and to be at home with the Lord" (5:8). His third choice was "to remain in the flesh" (Phil. 1:24).

In 2 Corinthians 5:6 Paul spoke of being at home in the body and absent from the Lord; in verse 8 he spoke of being absent from the body and at home with the Lord. Paul's ambition to please God, imperfectly on earth or perfectly in heaven, remained unchanged. Expressing that same breadth of devotion he affirmed, "For not one of us lives for himself, and not one dies for himself; for if we live, we live for the Lord, or if we die, we die for the Lord; therefore whether we live or die, we are the Lord's" (Rom. 14:7–8).

Some might assume that Paul's longing for heaven implied an indifference to his earthly body; that he espoused an antinomian view that it does not matter what one does with the sinful, physical body. Such a view would have been in harmony with the prevailing Greek philosophical dualism of his day that held the body to be the worthless and inconsequential prison of the soul. But Paul knew that he could serve God in his physical body in a way that would produce an eternal reward. Thus, his longing for heaven and his resurrection body made him even more careful about how he lived in this world. In 1 Corinthians 9:27 he wrote, "I discipline my body and make it my slave, so that, after I have preached to others, I myself will not be disqualified." He admonished the Romans, "Present your bodies a living and holy sacrifice, acceptable to God, which is your spiritual service of worship" (Rom. 12:1). Paul's ambition to please God in this life or the life to come demonstrates the broad scope of his devotion to the Lord.

PAUL'S DEEPEST MOTIVE

For we must all appear before the judgment seat of Christ, so that each one may be recompensed for his deeds in the body, according to what he has done, whether good or bad. (5:10)

Driving Paul's noble ambition was the knowledge that there would be a penetrating uncovering of the depths of his heart by the Lord Himself. That would take place in the future when believers "must all appear before the judgment seat of Christ." The strong terms "must" and "all" stress the inevitability and comprehensiveness of this event. That knowledge produced in Paul strong motivation to please God in this life.

"Appear" comes from the Greek *phaneroō,* meaning "to make manifest," "to make clear," "to make visible," or "to reveal." Commenting on the meaning of *phaneroō,* Philip Hughes writes, "To be made manifest means not just to appear, but to be laid bare, stripped of every outward façade of respectability, and openly revealed in the full and true reality of one's character."[3] Some have argued that the believers' secret motives and heart attitudes will be made manifest to the holy angels; there is, however, no biblical support for such speculation. Others hold that the disclosure of which Paul writes will be to other believers, a view also without biblical support. Believers will be too preoccupied with the unveiling of their own deeds to pay attention to the revealing of others' deeds. Nor do believers' hearts need to be made manifest to the omniscient God, who already knows every detail of their lives.

In that day, the full truth about their lives, character, and deeds will be made clear to each believer. Each will discover the real verdict on his or her ministry, service, and motives. All hypocrisy and pretense will be stripped away; all temporal matters with no eternal significance will vanish like wood, hay, and stubble, and only what is to be rewarded as eternally valuable will be left. First Samuel 16:7 declares that "God sees not as man sees, for man looks at the outward appearance, but the Lord looks at the heart." "There is no creature hidden from His sight," the writer of Hebrews adds, "but all things are open and laid bare to the eyes of Him with whom we have to do" (Heb. 4:13). The true assessment of the work God has done in and through believers will be disclosed on that day.

Believers will not be judged for sin at the judgment seat of Christ. Every sin of every believer was judged at the Cross, when God "made Him who knew no sin to be sin on our behalf, so that we might become the righteousness of God in Him" (2 Cor. 5:21). At the cross "Christ redeemed us from the curse of the Law, having become a curse for us" (Gal. 3:13). As our substitute, "He Himself bore our sins in His body on the cross, so that we might die to sin and live to righteousness" (1 Peter 2:24); "He, having offered one sacrifice for sins for all time, sat down at the right hand of God" (Heb. 10:12; cf. Eph. 1:7; 4:32; 1 John 2:1–2). Because of His atoning sacrifice on our behalf, "There is now no condemnation for those who are in Christ Jesus. . . . Who is the one who condemns? Christ Jesus is He who died, yes, rather, who was raised, who is at the right hand of God, who also intercedes for us" (Rom. 8:1, 34).

But though salvation is not by works, works are the inevitable result of true salvation. Hughes comments:

> It is worth remembering that a passage like this shows that, so far from there being discord, there is an essential agreement between the teaching of Paul and that of James on the subject of faith and works. The justification of the sinner, it is true, is by faith in Christ and not by works of his own; but the hidden root of faith must bring forth the visible fruit of good works. This fruit is expected by Christ, for it brings glory to the Father and is evidence to the world of the dynamic reality of divine grace. And it is especially in the bearing of *much* fruit that the Father is glorified (Jn. 15:8).[4]

In its simplest definition, the Greek word *bēma*, which is translated "judgment seat," describes a place reached by steps, or a platform. The Septuagint (the Greek translation of the Old Testament) uses it that way in Nehemiah 8:4. In Greek culture, *bēma* referred to the elevated platform on which victorious athletes received their crowns, much like the medal stand in the modern Olympic games. In the New Testament it was used of the judgment seats of Pilate (Matt. 27:19; John 19:13), Herod (Acts 12:21), and Festus (Acts 25:6, 10, 17). There was also a *bēma* at Corinth, where unbelieving Jews unsuccessfully accused Paul before the Roman proconsul Gallio (Acts 18:12, 16, 17). A person was brought before a *bēma* to have his or her deeds examined, in a judicial sense, for indictment or exoneration, or for the purpose of recognizing and rewarding some achievement.

Writing to the Romans of this same event, Paul described it as "the judgment seat [*bēma*] of God" (Rom. 14:10). God the Father is the ultimate Judge, but He has "given all judgment to the Son" (John 5:22). Paul Barnett notes,

> A parallel passage—"we shall all stand before the judgment seat of God" (Rom. 14:10)—implies an identity of function of Christ and God; God judges and Christ judges. The NT often refers to Christ as God's appointed judge, appropriate to his role as Son of Man, as in Dan. 7:13, 14, 26–27 (e.g., John 5:22, 27; 9:39; Matt. 25:31–32; Acts 10:42; 17:31; cf. Rev. 20:11–15).[5]

The phrase "each one" stresses the personal nature of believers' judgment; it is an individual, not a collective, judgment. Its purpose, as noted above, is not judicial; it is that every believer "may be recompensed for his deeds in the body." "Recompensed" translates a form of the verb *komizō*, which means "to receive back what is due"—whether punishment for a criminal, or reward for one to be honored. When believers stand before the Lord Jesus Christ they will be recompensed for the deeds they have done "in the body" (cf. Rev. 22:12). Therefore, they cannot disregard their bodies, or treat them with contempt in some antinomian or dualistic fashion. Instead, they are to "present [their] bodies a living and holy sacrifice, acceptable to God, which is [their] spiritual service of worship" (Rom. 12:1). Things done in the body do have potential eternal value (cf. Matt. 6:19–21).

The use of the word "bad" does not indicate that believers' judgment is a judgment on sin, since all their sin has already been judged in Christ. The contrast between good and bad is not one between moral good and moral evil. "Bad" does not translate *kakos* or *ponēros*, the words for moral evil, but *phaulos*, which means "worthless," or "useless." Richard C. Trench writes that *phaulos*

THE BELIEVER'S WALK WITH CHRIST

"contemplates evil under another aspect, not so much that either of active or passive malignity, but that rather of its good-for-nothingness, the impossibility of any true gain coming from it."[6] *Phaulos* describes those mundane things that inherently are neither of eternal value nor sinful, such as taking a walk, going shopping, taking a drive in the country, pursuing an advanced degree, moving up the corporate ladder, painting pictures, or writing poetry. Those morally neutral things will be judged when believers stand before the judgment seat of Christ. If they were done with a motive to glorify God, they will be considered good. If they were pursued for selfish interests, they will be considered bad.

The clearest definition of the difference between good and bad (worthless) things is in 1 Corinthians 3:11–15:

> For no man can lay a foundation other than the one which is laid, which is Jesus Christ. Now if any man builds on the foundation with gold, silver, precious stones, wood, hay, straw, each man's work will become evident; for the day will show it because it is to be revealed with fire, and the fire itself will test the quality of each man's work. If any man's work which he has built on it remains, he will receive a reward. If any man's work is burned up, he will suffer loss; but he himself will be saved, yet so as through fire.

The only foundation of the Christian life is the Lord Jesus Christ (cf. 1 Peter 2:6–8), but believers must build on that foundation, as Peter exhorted:

> But also for this very reason, giving all diligence, add to your faith virtue, to virtue knowledge, to knowledge self-control, to self-control perseverance, to perseverance godliness, to godliness brotherly kind-

ness, and to brotherly kindness love. For if these things are yours and
abound, you will be neither barren nor unfruitful in the knowledge
of our Lord Jesus Christ. For he who lacks these things is shortsight-
ed, even to blindness, and has forgotten that he was cleansed from his
old sins. Therefore, brethren, be even more diligent to make your call
and election sure, for if you do these things you will never stumble.
(2 Peter 1:5–10 NKJV)

Believers build for eternity not with "wood, hay, or straw,"
but with "gold, silver, [and] precious stones." The latter are valuable, permanent, and indestructible and will survive the fire of
judgment; the former, though not evil, are worthless and combus-
tible. They illustrate things with no lasting, eternal value. The fire,
symbolizing judgment, will consume them in that day when "each
man's work will become evident." Believers will only be rewarded
for deeds with motives that please and glorify the Lord.

As he walked by faith, and not by sight, Paul's longing for heav-
en did not cause him to act irresponsibly or unfaithfully here on
earth; it did just the opposite. His eager anticipation for the future
fueled his earnest ambition in this life to be pleasing to Christ in
everything.

NOTES

Chapter 2: Walking as a New Person

1. "The X-Rated Economy," *Forbes*, September 18, 1978, 81–92.

2. Walter Bauer, *A Greek–English Lexicon of the New Testament*, trans. and ed. W. F. Arndt and F. W. Gingrich. 5th ed. (Chicago: Univ. of Chicago, 1958), 490.

3. John Eadie, *A Commentary on the Greek Text of the Epistle of Paul to the Ephesians* (London: Forgotten Books, 2012), 351.

Chapter 3: Walking in Newness of Life

1. John Newton, *Out of the Depths: An Autobiography* (Chicago: Moody, n.d.), 151.

2. Donald Grey Barnhouse, *Romans*, vol. 3 (Grand Rapids: Eerdmans, 1961), 2:12.

3. Kenneth S. Wuest, *Romans in the Greek New Testament* (Grand Rapids: Eerdmans, 1955), 96–97.

4. Charles Hodge, *Commentary on the Epistle to the Romans* (Grand Rapids: Eerdmans, n.d.), 195.

5. Handley Moule, *The Epistle to the Romans* (London: Picketing & Inglis, n.d.), 160–61.

6. John Murray, *Principles of Conduct* (Grand Rapids: Eerdmans, 1957), see 211–19.

7. Moule, *The Epistle to the Romans*, 164.

8. D. Martyn Lloyd-Jones, *Romans: An Exposition of Chapter 6* (Grand Rapids: Zondervan, 1973), 64.

9. Ibid., 26–27.

Chapter 4: Walking by the Spirit

1. For a more detailed study of this concept, see "Be Filled with the Spirit" in my commentary *Ephesians*, The MacArthur New Testament Commentary (Chicago: Moody, 1986), 245–69.

2. Richard C. Trench, *Synonyms of the New Testament,* (Grand Rapids: Eerdmans, 1953; repr., n. c.: Aeterna, 2010), 110.

Chapter 5: Walking in Obedience

1. Thomas Brooks, *Heaven on Earth: A Treatise on Christian Assurance* (reprint; Edinburgh: Banner of Truth, 1982), 14.

2. Ibid., 11.

3. Ibid., 15, 11.

4. See John MacArthur, *The Gospel According to the Apostles* (Nashville: Nelson, 1993, 2000), chap. 10.

5. As cited in J.C. Ryle, *Holiness* (1877, 1879; repr., Moscow, Idaho: Charles Nolan Publishers, 2002), 123.

6. Ibid., n. 1.

7. John Stott, *The Epistles of John*, The Tyndale New Testament Commentaries (Grand Rapids: Eerdmans, 1964), 91; italics in original.

Chapter 6: Walking in Love

1. George MacDonald, *Robert Falconer* (London: Hurst and Blackett, 1868), 125–26.

Chapter 7: Walking in Wisdom

1. Cited in David Russell Schilling,"Knowledge Doubles Every 12 Months, Soon to Be Every 12 Hours," *Industry Tap into News*, April 19, 2013, http://www.industrytap.com/knowledge-doubling-every-12-months-soon-to-be-every-12-hours/3950

2. Ibid.

3. Ibid.

4. Pausanias, *Description of Greece*, vol .2, book 5.14.9, trans. W. H. S. Jones (Cambridge, MA: Harvard University Press, n.d.); http://www.theoi.com/Daimon/Kairos.html. Pausanias, a Roman traveler, wrote this travelogue about Ancient Greece in the second century A.D., describing its culture, buildings, and myths (includes Roman poetry).

5. The story of Kefa Sempangi is told in F. Kefa Sempangi, *A Distant Grief* (Glendale, CA: Regal, 1979; repr., Eugene, OR: Wipf and Stock, 2006).

Chapter 8: Walking in the Truth

1. *D. Martin Luthers Werke, Kritische Gesamtausgabe. Briefwechesel*, 18 vols. (Weimar, Germany: Verlag Hermann Bohlaus Nachfolger, 1930–1985) 3:81; emphasis added.

2. Cf. Alfred Plummer, *The Epistles of St. John,* The Cambridge Bible for Schools and Colleges (Cambridge: Cambridge Univ., 1911), 175.

3. Other New Testament passages which variously translate *elektos* as "appointed," "chose," "called," or predestined," are Acts 13:48; Rom. 8:28–30; Eph. 1:4–5, 11; 2 Thess. 2:13; 2 Tim. 1:9; and James 2:5.

4. John R. W. Stott, *The Epistles of John,* The Tyndale New Testament Commentaries (Grand Rapids: Eerdmans, 1975), 206.

Chapter 9: Walking by Faith

1. Quoted in John Blanchard, *Truth for Life* (Welwyn: Evangelical Press, 1986), 179.

2. Quoted in J. Oswald Sanders, *Spiritual Leadership*, rev. ed. (Chicago: Moody, 1980), 14.

3. Philip E. Hughes, *The Second Epistle to the Corinthians* (Grand Rapids: Eerdmans, 1992), 180.

4. Ibid., 183.

5. Paul Barnett, *The Second Epistle to the Corinthians*, The New International Commentary on the New Testament (Grand Rapids: Eerdmans, 1997), 275 n. 45.

6. Richard C. Trench, *Synonyms of the New Testament* (Grand Rapids: Eerdmans, 1953; repr. 1983), 317.

ACKNOWLEDGMENTS

Our thanks to Nathan Busenitz in gathering and organizing material from various books in the thirty-three volume MacArthur New Testament Bible Commentary for this book in the John MacArthur Study Series. Nathan also added new introductions and material to several of the chapters.

Our special thanks to the team at Moody Publishers, particularly senior editor Jim Vincent and acquiring editor Drew Dyck. Jim updated sources and examples and tightened the text in key places; Drew had valuable suggestions throughout.

PULPIT OF **JOHN CALVIN** | ST. PIERRE CATHEDRAL | GENEVA, SWITZERLAND

WE PREACH **CHRIST**

THE MASTER'S SEMINARY